LIFELONG VITALITY

Twelve Pathways
to Ageing Youthfully

LILI-ANN KRIEGLER

First published by Ultimate World Publishing 2024
Copyright © 2024 Lili-Ann Kriegler

ISBN

Paperback: 978-1-923255-75-3
Ebook: 978-1-923255-76-0

Lili-Ann Kriegler has asserted her rights under the Copyright, Designs and Patents Act 1988 to be identified as the author of this work. The information in this book is based on the author's experiences and opinions. The publisher specifically disclaims responsibility for any adverse consequences which may result from use of the information contained herein. Permission to use information has been sought by the author. Any breaches will be rectified in further editions of the book.

All rights reserved. No part of this publication may be reproduced, stored in or introduced into a retrieval system, or transmitted in any form, or by any means (electronic, mechanical, photocopying, recording or otherwise) without the prior written permission of the author. Any person who does any unauthorised act in relation to this publication may be liable to criminal prosecution and civil claims for damages. Enquiries should be made through the publisher.

Cover design: Ultimate World Publishing
Layout and typesetting: Ultimate World Publishing
Editor: Marinda Wilkinson

Ultimate World Publishing
Diamond Creek,
Victoria Australia 3089
www.writeabook.com.au

Testimonials

Lili-Ann has written an enlightening and practical guide that offers a refreshing perspective on ageing youthfully. She skilfully blends research with actionable advice, creating a roadmap for readers to embrace life and take personal responsibility for their youthfulness. The inclusion of real-life examples and personal anecdotes adds depth and relatability to the content, making readers feel understood and connected.

Lifelong Vitality – Twelve Pathways to Ageing Youthfully is an invaluable resource for anyone looking to navigate the ageing process with grace, vitality and purpose.
          Diane Bourke – Education Consultant and Past School Principal

Lifelong Vitality – Twelve Pathways to Ageing Youthfully is a practical guide that everyone, regardless of age, should read. The book is filled with valuable common sense, which is increasingly rare today. The emphasis on embracing responsibility early in life is particularly noteworthy, as it sets the foundation for successfully navigating the years ahead.
This is an engaging read with solid ideas; I recommend it to people of all ages.
          Fran Winckworth – Past School Principal

Lifelong Vitality – Twelve Pathways to Ageing Youthfully is well-written and easy to read. Its interesting content and thoughtful perspectives keep your attention, and the quotes and references are a nice touch.

Candice Kriegler – Veterinarian and Daughter

Lifelong Vitality – Twelve Pathways to Ageing Youthfully resonates deeply with many of my experiences. The pathways outlined in the book reflect valuable practices and insights that align closely with maintaining health and staying active. The emphasis on family life and shared meals mirrors my values.

It is a meaningful and engaging read, and I look forward to seeing it in print.

John Crigler – Civil Engineer
Principal, Woodline Primary School, Geelong

Dedication

This book is dedicated to:

Pierre, my exceptional husband, whose love, support, insights and patience are the wind beneath my wings.

To my talented children, Sean and Candice, and your partners, Judy and Eric, your enthusiastic interest in all my endeavours – no matter how wild – inspires me.

To my grandson, Ivar, who is the bringer of joy.

To my late parents, Bob and Bee, whose care and unwavering encouragement instilled in me a deep love of education.

To my siblings, Helene and Martin, whose accomplishments stand as a testament to our shared foundation.

To my friends and network, whose steadfast support and camaraderie have been a constant source of strength. Thank you for being part of this incredible journey.

And to everyone who has shared this journey, thank you for giving me a sense of belonging.

Lili-Ann respects the Traditional Owners and Custodians of the land of the Kulin Nation groups, the Boonwurrung and Bunurong people, where I live, learn, and work.

Contents

Testimonials	3
Dedication	5
Introduction	9
Pathway One: Nurturing Vitality in Childhood	13
Pathway Two: Taking Personal Responsibility Toward Youthfulness	15
Pathway Three: The Power of Human Connection	19
Pathway Four: The Lifelong Impact of Education	31
Pathway Five: Nutrition for Lifelong Health	37
Pathway Six: Exercise – The Time Machine to Youthful Energy	43
Pathway Seven: Style, Beauty and Body Care	49
Pathway Eight: Self-Care and Self-Protection	79
Pathway Nine: Finding Purpose and Energy in Work	87
Pathway Ten: Unlocking Creativity for Vitality	93
Pathway Eleven: Fun and Relaxation	97
Pathway Twelve: Financial Literacy for a Secure Future	101
Final Words	107
References	111
About the Author	113

Introduction

> 'Nature gives you the face you have at twenty;
> it is up to you to merit the face you have at fifty.'
>
> **Coco Chanel**

I agree with Gabrielle Bonheur Chanel when she says you earn your looks at fifty. But ageing youthfully goes beyond just appearances. It's about how you think, feel, move, act, work, communicate and connect with the world around you. Ageing well isn't something you can suddenly achieve as you hit middle age. You can't simply rush to get younger. However, the empowering truth is, that you can achieve it through the choices and decisions you make every day, from early youth onwards.

In this book, I introduce twelve pathways to ageing youthfully. Each chapter stands independently, but they are all interconnected. For instance, while I discuss work and finance separately, work impacts your financial gains, allowing you to invest in the nutrition, exercise and health care needed to stay vibrant and youthful. As you read, I hope you recognise the holistic connections between each pathway.

What comes to mind when you think about growing old? When I was eighteen, I mourned my mother's fortieth birthday! Now, I see forty-year-olds as spring chickens. As I've grown, I've met people who've embarked on new ventures at ages I once thought were reserved for the frail and worn out. Take Emily Kame Kngwarreye, a First Nations artist who began painting in her late seventies. Despite working in a remote part of the Simpson Desert, she became one of Australia's most celebrated artists in the last decade of her life.

Her story is not just inspiring; it's a testament to challenging traditional views on ageing. Conventional views of what defines the stages of life are outdated. We live longer and know enough to maintain our vibrance for decades. Whilst ageing presents its challenges, they don't have to define us. We can navigate these difficulties and reinvent ourselves many times as we journey through late life. I hope the notion shared throughout this book, that people remain productive well into old age, will inspire you as much as it does me.

Research shows that feeling grateful for what you have, rather than focusing on what you don't, boosts happiness. Take time to appreciate the often-overlooked aspects of your life that enhance its quality. A positive mindset about ageing isn't merely a belief; it's crucial for feeling younger. In this book, I share tools and insights to help you cultivate this mindset and age youthfully. Remember, your mindset is a powerful tool in your journey towards graceful ageing.

Early Inspiration

As a child, I loved caravanning with my parents and siblings. Our holidays were usually spent at campsites by the sea. My parents believed in everyone pulling their weight, so my sister, Helene, and I had our chores. My brother, a busy four-year-old, was more into hammering tent pegs than anything else. One of our tasks was washing dishes in a communal camp kitchen. One evening, when I was eleven and becoming self-conscious, we met a woman whose arms were immersed in soap suds up to her elbows. She was friendly and struck up a conversation with us. She was over sixty and had been a professional dancer in her youth. Tall, slim and elegant, her grey hair was neatly pinned up. Her posture captivated me most; she moved with such grace that I aspired to be as graceful as she was at sixty (even though I never thought I'd reach that age). She was a living example of someone whose biological age was younger than her chronological age. The book *Life Force* (Diamandis, Robbins, & Hariri, 2022) highlights that our biology can be younger than our actual age.

Having surpassed sixty, I must admit that ageing has indeed occurred! I'm not as tall as the dishwashing dancer, nor do I have her flawless posture, but her early influence has been a constant inspiration. I don't look twenty or thirty anymore – no-one can – but I've made the most of what I could to age youthfully. This is what I wish to share with you in this book.

Disclaimer: The views in this book are based on personal experiences rather than specific empirical research. Nonetheless, my choices have been informed by established studies and research on health and ageing. I write with the understanding that everyone faces different challenges and circumstances, hoping that the insights shared may help you make choices that lead to a fulfilling experience of graceful ageing.

All content within this book is intended for informational purposes only. It is not intended to be a substitute for professional medical advice. Always seek the advice of a medical practitioner with any questions you may have regarding your health.

PATHWAY ONE

Nurturing Vitality in Childhood

> 'There can be no keener revelation of a society's soul than how it treats its children.'
>
> **Nelson Mandela**

The Chinese bamboo tree vividly illustrates early childhood development. Although it appears to stand still for years, it secretly builds an intricate root system underground. This hidden growth enables the bamboo to quickly shoot up to astonishing heights. This illustrates that our most formative growth sometimes occurs out of sight, and the foundations laid in early childhood are critical to future success.

Life can seem like a lottery – some children are born into more nurturing environments than others. I was fortunate to grow up in a supportive and loving family. Having a stable and supportive home environment is a privilege. I was lucky to experience this – well-fed, cared for and guided through education and life's joys by a loving family. This nurturing environment was instrumental in shaping my path. I encourage you to use your influence to create similar favourable conditions for the children in your life. Providing security, proper nutrition, a sense of belonging and educational opportunities is vital. Wellbeing and lasting success are built on genetics but also on the strength of our early experiences and the support we receive.

My siblings and I were blessed with a caring environment. We were well-nourished, supported in our studies, and encouraged to explore and connect with the world. Our activities included library visits, family outings and sleepovers with grandparents without the distractions of digital devices. In today's world, where digital distractions are prevalent, finding a balance is challenging.

If you didn't benefit from a stable, nurturing environment, remember you can redefine your future. Your brain and body are adaptable, and you can transform your path with deliberate, positive changes. It's never too late to cultivate new habits, embrace enriching experiences and build a fulfilling life.

Actions to reshape your future are always within your grasp.

PATHWAY TWO

Taking Personal Responsibility Toward Youthfulness

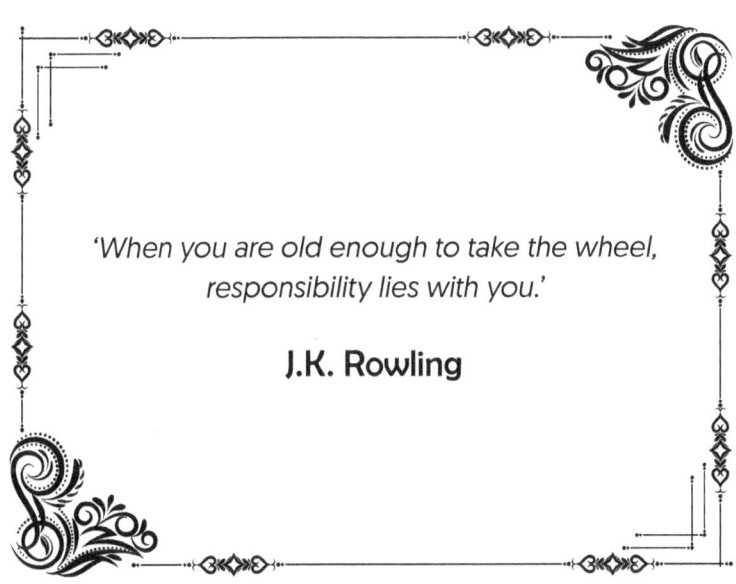

'When you are old enough to take the wheel, responsibility lies with you.'

J.K. Rowling

Legend has it that an old Cherokee grandfather taught his grandson about life through a parable. He said, 'A fight is going on inside me, a terrible fight between two wolves. One is evil – he is anger, envy, sorrow, regret, greed, arrogance, self-pity, guilt, resentment, inferiority, lies, false pride, superiority and ego.' He continued, 'The other is good – he is joy, peace, love, hope, responsibility, serenity, humility, kindness, benevolence, empathy, generosity, truth, compassion and faith. The same fight is happening inside you – and every other person, too.'

Curious and contemplative, the grandson asked his grandfather, 'Which wolf will win?' The old Cherokee replied, 'The one you feed.'

This tale encapsulates the essence of personal responsibility. While we may not always have control over external circumstances, the power to shape our lives often resides in our choices. We can guide ourselves toward a path of vitality and youthfulness by nurturing the 'good wolf' of positivity, love and commitment. It reminds us that we are not merely passengers in our lives but drivers of our destinies.

It's important to acknowledge that some individuals face life circumstances where their ability to exercise personal responsibility is severely restricted. For those who struggle with systemic barriers, personal limitations or profound challenges, the path to taking responsibility may seem fraught with obstacles. Even small steps towards taking control can be incredibly significant and worthy of recognition.

If you have choices, embracing responsibility can yield lifelong benefits. Blaming others for your challenges is often unproductive because it relinquishes your power to effect change. Instead, focusing on what you can control – your actions and reactions – empowers you to create a more fulfilling life.

Taking responsibility isn't a trait that magically appears; it can be cultivated at any stage of life. It starts with simple practices, like involving children in household chores and instilling a sense of accountability from an early age.

It benefits children if they are given responsibility early in life. In our home, as inferred earlier, we were given chores. After a meal, we would help to clear dishes, wash and dry, sweep the floor and reset the room. I remember being as tall as the vacuum cleaner when I started using it to help my mother. And we helped in the garden. I loved watering with the hose because I could create the water stream into jewels of light above my head. There is great satisfaction in building up a massive pile of weeds, especially if they have been successfully pulled out by the roots.

As teenagers, we took on holiday jobs that further developed our self-belief and taught us to navigate different work environments. This early exposure to responsibility builds a foundation of self-assurance and life skills that benefit us throughout adulthood.

Community service is another avenue where responsibility can enhance our sense of success and self-worth. Helping others and contributing to the wellbeing of our communities enriches our lives and strengthens our connection to the world.

But how does all this contribute to feeling youthful? It's about cultivating a mindset of success and self-assurance.

A considerable aspect of taking responsibility is setting goals for yourself. When you visualise yourself as you would like to be in the future, it is easier to take the steps towards that goal. You go through the hoops like someone who will be that person in the future. Your visions inform your identity. No dream comes true in an instant.

Part of your responsibility is to create habits that sustain your dreams. I love James Clear's book, *Atomic Habits*. I have used the advice to implement habit stacking. You add one small habit to another, making it easy and automatic. For example, I have an exercise routine called the 'bare minimum'. It takes seven minutes. I do it when my bath is running. And it's over so quickly it's not a chore. However, the benefits over time are remarkable for my strength and flexibility.

Goals affect all areas of life: self-management, education, career, relationships, hobbies, travel, financial comfort, family life and more. As you achieve goals in one area, the benefits spill over into other areas. Goals integrate your life and are the basis of your success.

They say that what can't be measured can't be improved. Recently, we have gained access to many ways to measure and track goals. Digital food diaries and calorie counters, exercise trackers, online journals, online planners and event design platforms have made knowing where we are in our journey easier.

But to use them, we must have the imagination to see what is possible. Many people calibrate their goals according to their circumstances growing up and set their ambitions accordingly. Be courageous and innovative and design a giant canvas for your life. Do research, find mentors who guide you, develop a learning pathway and follow your dream. Choose your own life; don't let others decide it for you.

Some excellent self-help books can help you be more responsible, including *Eat That Frog! Get More of the Important Things Done—Today!* by Brian Tracy and *The Five Second Rule* by Mel Robbins.

The greater the responsibility you take for yourself, your earning power and your environment, the more likely you are to create a successful life trajectory. When you experience life success, you are likely more able to cope with the stresses you encounter. Stress is a significant factor in ageing, and your health will benefit if you manage it well.

Responsibility is essential on the road to life's success (Shaver & Mikulincer, 2012).

PATHWAY THREE

The Power of Human Connection

'All you need is one person who understands you completely, believes in you and makes you feel loved for what you are, to enable you to unfold the miraculous YOU.'

Drishti Bablani

The Joy of Family Life

Being part of a loving family is the pinnacle of connection. In our era, there are many kinds of families and relationships. Not everyone chooses to have children. In my experience, my life partner and children have been incredible sources of joy and belonging.

Life Partner
We are privileged if we find a loving partner with whom to share our journey. Whether this is marriage or a different long-term relationship, having a partner to face the world with enables you to share the load.

I love the words of Kahlil Gibran on marriage, and I think they apply to any long-term partnership:

> *'... stand together yet not too near together:*
>
> *For the pillars of the temple stand apart,*
>
> *And the oak tree and the cypress grow*
>
> *not in each other's shadow.'*

Gibran's words highlight the importance of allowing one another to grow. A great partnership is built on love, intimacy, respect, support, patience and loyalty. Then, add a pinch of spice and a large dash of humour. Laughter and the art of communication go a long way to creating a successful partnership. Being each other's protector, defender and cheerleader cements ties. The stability of a partner means that stressors and problems are shared. When someone has your back, you can weather storms, achieve goals and grow economically. All of this helps you to retain a youthful fortitude.

Family Ties

Having a family further enriches lives. Many people decide not to have children, and everyone has the right to decide. But if you choose to have children, a few things make it easier. A most important aspect of family life is for the parental figures, whoever they are, to be on the same page about bringing up their children. Even if they disagree, it's best if they discuss and resolve their differences and decide what they will do. A united front makes it easier to set boundaries and affirm family values.

Children are a joy, but they are not all sunshine and roses. There will be challenging times. However, showing them the same respect, love and support that you show your partner will make the family unit strong and resilient. I recently wrote about this in great detail in my book *Roots and Wings – A Parents' Guide to Learning and Communication with Children to Forge a Family with Mettle*.

I am fortunate to have married my husband, Pierre, when I was twenty-two, and we've been together ever since. Our son, Sean, and daughter, Candice, are the lights of our lives. They have continued building solid foundations with their life partners, and I couldn't be happier with who they have become.

Were there tough times? Certainly, but it's essential to stand firm and fight for what you believe in. And that goes for both generations. As parents, we set expectations, but sometimes we also need to bend.

Kahlil Gibran says about children:

> *'You may strive to be like them but seek*
> *not to make them like you.*
> *For life goes not backward nor tarries with yesterday.*
> *You are the bows from which your children as living arrows*
> *are sent forth.'*

Individuals have the right to forge their paths. If you create beautiful family relationships, they become a golden thread that stretches into the future.

Tips for Family Unity

Have a Family Emblem and Family Motto
Our family chose the dolphin as an emblem for several reasons. Dolphins are a blend of intelligence, wisdom and social harmony. Known for their problem-solving abilities and cooperative nature within pods, dolphins symbolise the importance of unity and friendship within the family. As protectors and guides, dolphins represent resilience and the ability to navigate life's challenges. Their playful and joyful nature underscores the importance of enjoying life together as a family.

Our motto is, 'We may not have it all together, but when we're together, we have it all.'

Family Celebrations and Rituals
Rituals and family celebrations strengthen ties and a sense of belonging. Our family has a Spring Dinner each year. We collect jasmine and make crowns. Even as adults, our children insist on wearing the crowns as they enjoy a traditional lamb roast dinner. Explore and value your familial and cultural traditions for the close bonds they create for you and your loved ones.

I recently wrote a recipe book with all our favourite recipes. Gathering around a table and eating food you love with those you love is often where the fondest memories are made.

Sibling Tribalry
Rather than sibling rivalry, try to promote sibling tribalism, where everyone works together on team goals and supports each person's goals. My

brother lives in the UK, my sister lives in Spain, and I live in Australia, far-flung from our roots in South Africa. Yet, we maintain strong bonds and are often one another's sounding boards and advisors. It is comforting to know that despite the tyranny of distance, we can depend on each other. Fortunately, my two adult children have grown into respectful siblings who support each other and combine their expertise for better outcomes.

Human connection weaves our stories together in the tapestry of life. From socialisation and gratitude to communication and respect, the power of connection is immeasurable (Stiles, 2021) (Martino, Pegg, & Pegg Frates, 2015).

Beyond the Family

How a Banana Made a Difference
Andrew Griffiths, an Australian-based entrepreneur and author, describes an incident on a plane when a man boarded late and sat beside him. The man was out of breath, flustered and didn't speak much English. Once airborne, Andrew opened his bag and pulled out two bananas. He offered one to the old timer, who stopped, looked him in the eye and got teary.

In broken English, he said he was an exceptionally long way from home and felt very alone, unsettled and afraid. At that moment, a stranger was offering him food. He suddenly felt that everything would be okay.

Andrew's anecdote illustrates the reality of life. We are often so busy, so preoccupied, so distracted that most of us don't even stop to make eye contact with other people, let alone offer a simple act of kindness. When we are kind, the life we change the most is our own.

Human connection influences the quality of our lives and overall wellbeing. From emotional support to physical health benefits, our connections with others are pivotal in shaping our identity and contribution to those around us.

The Essence of Socialisation

Whether you are an extrovert or introvert, you can benefit from strategies for being a better socialiser. Developing social skills allows you to build bridges with people from all levels of society, creating a sense of belonging and unity. Social skills are formed from an early age.

School is where social competence and networks are made or broken. It's imperative to keep open communication and listen to youngsters discussing their relationships. Self-identity and self-worth are bolstered or bashed at school, and the experiences can have lasting positive or adverse effects.

Fortunately, social skills can be learned, and there is a wide variety of sources for gaining more social aptitude and even developing leadership skills. Daniel Goleman's groundbreaking book *Emotional Intelligence* shows how emotional intelligence can be learned (Goleman, 1995). He says, 'All boats are lifted on a rising tide.' People can learn empathy and how to interact in a respectful and positive way in relation to others.

There are simple strategies that can oil the social waters.

Introduction Tips
It's helpful to others to introduce yourself by name as you shake hands or say hello. This will help those who know you and may have forgotten your name. If you've forgotten someone else's, the quickest, most painless route is to apologise immediately, have them remind you and get on with things.

Express Gratitude: Strengthening Bonds
Gratitude nurtures connections. Simply saying 'thank you' and expressing gratitude can deepen relationships. Research shows that people who feel and express gratitude are happier and more successful than those who don't. A powerful mindset is to frame things in a positive light. Rather than think a social event will be tedious or difficult, think about how lucky you are to have the opportunity to go out and meet people. Rather than say, 'I have to', say, 'I get to'. Those who are mobile and financially able to socialise are the lucky ones. A fantastic book on this topic is Carol Dweck's *Mindset* (Dweck, 2017).

Don't Take People for Granted
It's easy to take others for granted if you are used to their place and contribution to your life. But everyone likes to feel appreciated. So, remember to tell them regularly that they are essential to you.

Team Player: Collaborative Spirit
Being a team player, whether in sports, work or life, teaches the value of cooperation and unity. This lesson extends beyond the field or office into your daily interactions. Teamwork contributes to everyone's success in the family.

The Art of Conversation and Connection
Effective communication is the cornerstone of meaningful connections. Learning to converse with others, engage in active listening and express yourself clearly develops deeper bonds. Whether talking to a taxi driver, a friend, a retailer or a royal, the art of conversation makes for enjoyable interactions. My son, Sean, did a personal development course in his early twenties. One of his challenges was to go into the centre of Melbourne and start a thousand conversations with random people on the street. At first, he found it nerve-wracking. However, after a time, he learned many hooks and techniques for drawing people into talking to him. One of my strategies when I don't know people at a cocktail party or conference is to join a group and say, 'Hello, I'm Lili, and I'm gatecrashing.' I've never been

thrown out of a group, and I've met lovely people. Finding connections, such as a shared interest in sport, a cultural tie, an opinion on a current event or discussing the weather, are great starters. I am often surprised by how deep conversations go when they are started respectfully, open-mindedly and open-heartedly.

Giving a Compliment: Appreciation
Who doesn't love a compliment? Yet, we are often awkward about accepting them. Someone says, 'What a lovely dress.' You say, 'Oh, this old thing?' Learn to take a compliment with grace. I once interviewed a young teacher for a role and complimented her on a professional portfolio she had brought along. Her face brightened, and she looked at me directly and said, 'Thank you.' I have tried to do that since then.

When talking about the accolades of others during conversations, think carefully about the impact on the listeners. Curiously, when you emphasise an absent person's strengths or qualities, the person you're talking to often feels diminished or not as good. At an elegant function, I once sat beside a gentleman talking about his daughter. But how he said it was, 'Like you, my daughter has made great strides in her education career.' This was such a lesson. I felt included, not diminished. So, I try to give inclusive compliments as often as I can.

Another simple and easy thing to do is compliment strangers. It will uplift their spirits and brighten their day.

Sense of Humour: Lightening the Mood
A sense of humour is a powerful tool for connecting with others. Laughter is a universal language that breaks down barriers and brings people together. You don't want the humour to be unkind or disrespectful. A saying goes that it is only funny if everyone is laughing. I find that highlighting my quirks and humorous stories allows others to share theirs for a laugh. Research shows that moods lift the instant the corners of your mouth go up, so practise smiling and laughing to generate

happiness. It makes you seem younger and more fun to be around. In his book *Laughter, the Best Medicine*, Robert Holden explores this in-depth (Holden, 1998).

Avoid Gossip
Gossip can be destructive to relationships. Try to behave about others' reputations and privacy as you would like them to treat you and yours.

Be Careful When Sharing Confidence
When you take someone into your confidence and share something you don't want to have spread any further, tell them. I usually say, 'I know you won't repeat this', and then share what I planned to say. This simple habit can avoid embarrassment or recriminations later.

Telling Stories: Sharing Experiences
Learning how to tell a compelling story allows us to connect with others on a personal level. Stories evoke empathy and create lasting connections. Stories are part of each family's culture and identity. They create a shared experience and sense of belonging. The more a person feels they belong, the more secure they are. The more secure they are, the more they will take on challenges. The more challenges they take on, the more they will achieve. A sense of belonging enriches lives.

Supportive Relationships: Give and Take
In our personal and professional relationships, being there to support others and relying on their support when needed is a vital aspect of connection. Someone's unsolicited kindness or support is invaluable when you are feeling down. Giving gifts, skills, food, help or kind words often makes the giver feel as good as the receiver.

Moais in the Blue Zones
There are blue zones on the planet where people live for as long as fifteen years more than the average for other areas. The Okinawa Islands in Japan are an example. Regular socialisation, good nutrition and

exercise were pinpointed as contributory factors. People enact the idea of Moais, lifelong friendship groups in these zones. Moais epitomises the longevity effect of community bonds. Elders in the community gather regularly, finding comfort and support in their enduring relationships. Beyond companionship, Moais aids in stress reduction and provides vital social connections. In times of need, these groups offer support, ensuring individuals navigate life's difficulties with the strength of their community beside them. Start building your circle early!

A Quick List:

Play: Balancing Competition
Learning to win and lose gracefully is a valuable lesson in human interaction. It teaches humility and the importance of fair play.

Equal Treatment: Valuing Every Individual
Treating everyone with respect and equality is fundamental to building connections. It's a practice that extends to all aspects of life.

Mentorship and Inspiration: Guiding Others
Being a mentor to those who seek guidance is a way to give back and strengthen connections. Inspiring oneself enables us to inspire others, creating a cycle of positive influence.

Gracious Gestures: Recognising Excellence
Acknowledging and telling others when they're doing great is a gesture that reinforces positive behaviour and creates an atmosphere of appreciation.

Politeness: A Universal Language
Politeness is a language that transcends borders and cultures. Treating all individuals you encounter courteously creates harmonious connections and respect.

Humility: Grounded in Reality
Never feeling superior to others is a practice of humility. Recognising that we're all equal humans paves the way for genuine connections.

The Silent Epidemic: Loneliness
Loneliness has been described as a silent epidemic affecting people across generations. Connecting with others, whether through friendships or community involvement, helps combat the isolating effects of loneliness.

The Digital Age: New Forms of Connection
The digital age has given us unprecedented ways to connect with others, from social media to video chats. These tools offer convenience but should complement, not replace, face-to-face interactions. Where screens sometimes dominate our interactions, remember that the true essence of human connection lies in the genuine, face-to-face moments that enrich our lives. Through our connections, we find purpose, joy and the enduring vitality of the human spirit.

Feeling connected and supported is good for our health and ultimately contributes to feeling younger and more energetic.

PATHWAY FOUR

The Lifelong Impact of Education

> 'The purpose of education
> is to turn mirrors into windows.'
>
> **Sydney J. Harris**

The World Bank Education Overview states:

> 'Education is a human right, a powerful driver of development, and one of the strongest instruments for reducing poverty and improving health, gender equality, peace and stability. It delivers large, consistent returns regarding income and is the most important factor to ensure equity and inclusion.'
> (World Bank, 2024)

A global figure illustrating the importance of education is Malala Yousafzai. A Pakistani activist for female education and the youngest Nobel Prize laureate, Malala staunchly advocated for girls' education in the Swat Valley. Malala's narrative highlights education's transformative influence and the human spirit's remarkable resilience. Malala's defiance against her Taliban adversaries underscores her belief in the power of education to transform individuals and society.

Education has been proven to have extensive life benefits and can completely alter a life trajectory. It opens career possibilities, leading to an extraordinary ability to afford all life has to offer. It extends far beyond the confines of a classroom. It's about embracing a journey of discovery and growth. Like Malala, I see education as a vehicle to transform individual lives, families, communities and even societies.

In each life, education is the pathway to success. The path may twist and turn, but education unlocks doors that would otherwise remain closed. It sharpens your talents, ignites creativity, and enables you to navigate the world's complexities. Each lesson and skill you learn expands your possibilities. Educated individuals can choose their path and become the architects of their future.

If education is essential for boys and men, it is doubly important for women. Multiple studies, including one by UNICEF (UNICEF, 2024), conclude that educating women results in extensive health, economic and social benefits. When women flourish, society flourishes.

They say that luck is where preparation meets opportunity. My lifelong privilege of access to education has been the foundation of personal growth and self-improvement. It has meant that when opportunities have come my way, even if slightly beyond my comfort zone, I've had the confidence to jump right in. Education has enriched my life and career from the earliest days of formal schooling to continual adult learning.

I've already forgotten most of the content stuff I learned at school. Who hasn't? But school teaches you invaluable general skills. Language, critical thinking, problem-solving and the basics of numbers are fundamental tools for navigating life's complexities. I wish they would add a curriculum stream for financial literacy, which is sadly lacking in most curricula.

Language and Literacy
Language skills underlie effective communication and cognitive abilities. Language gives you the ability to understand concepts and ideas. It fuels the intellect. Learning to express ideas eloquently and persuasively transcends age and enables you to engage in meaningful conversations with anyone, anywhere, from your friendly Uber driver to the King of England (if you were to meet him).

There are enormous benefits to having more than one language. Growing up in South Africa, I learned Afrikaans. I haven't used it since I emigrated to Australia, but the structure of Afrikaans helped me interpret other languages as I travelled. Plus, each language has a different worldview. Some concepts and ideas can't be translated.

If you are fortunate enough to be in a multilingual family, it is worth researching the best way to pass the languages on to your children. Findings suggest that if you are bilingual and have two parental figures in the family, it is best if each of them selects one of the languages in all their communication with their children.

Fluency in language helps in public speaking. This skill can be learned and evolved throughout life, enhancing your ability to connect with others, receive recognition and succeed in all life endeavours. In almost all roles in life, public speaking and excellent communication are significant assets. Indeed, they may make you upwardly mobile into leadership.

Life in Books
One of the simplest ways to bolster knowledge and personal development is to read widely. Books offer diverse perspectives and a wealth of knowledge. If you can discuss what is current, you instantly come across as more youthful. Audible books will transform your reading life if you're like me and don't have much time for reading. My car, named Honeybee, is a mobile university. I started listening to Audible books three years ago and have read over fifty books yearly while travelling in my car.

Reading books about babies and children offers insights into child development, parenting techniques and family dynamics.

Self-development books are invaluable companions. They explore personal growth, motivation and success strategies. There is no age limit for self-improvement.

Magazines can be excellent educational resources because of their niche topics and concise articles. They keep readers informed and engaged with the world around them.

Beauty books recommend skincare, grooming and overall self-care, empowering you to look and feel your best at any age.

Podcasts and YouTube Videos
There is a wealth of digital information available. At sixteen, my son built a computer called the *Blue Beast*. He researched how to assemble it on YouTube and ordered parts from everywhere, including Poland. While at university, my daughter built a double-storey snake enclosure for her diamond pythons, Honey and Zeke. Again, she learned design skills and methods from YouTube. I shuddered to watch her using the power saw, thankfully wearing eye protection … but the snakes were happy. They only escaped twice … and yes, they were found and returned to their enclosure.

The Arts
Engaging with the theatre and the arts invigorates the soul. Whether as a spectator or a participant, the arts ignite passion and inspire creativity and emotional expression. Film and television transport you to different worlds and cultures, enriching your understanding of human experience. Exploring music or learning an instrument keeps the brain agile and connects you with the universal language of melody and rhythm.

Travel and Student Exchanges
Despite the burgeoning online information, travel and student exchanges hold immense value in broadening perspectives and enriching lives. By immersing yourself in different cultures and environments, you gain a deeper understanding of the world, encouraging empathy and open-mindedness. These experiences promote personal growth and adaptability, skills crucial in an increasingly globalised society. Additionally, the connections made during such exchanges often evolve into lifelong friendships and professional networks, emphasising the adage that success frequently hinges on who you know rather than what you know. These relationships can provide valuable support, opportunities and insights long after the journey has ended.

In addition to these traditional forms of education, keeping up with trends, music, world news, and technology will make you seem younger and more in touch with the spirit of the times.

Education is more than accumulating knowledge; it's a means to maintain youthful confidence and engage with others in any social environment. It helps you stand taller physically, emotionally and intellectually. Dedicating time and effort to expanding knowledge and skills will pave the way for a successful and fulfilling life.

Looking to the future, education is poised for exciting transformation. With the rise of artificial intelligence, we're on the brink of personalised learning experiences that adapt to each student's unique needs. AI could identify learning gaps and offer tailored support, making education more responsive and effective. Digital tools and online platforms are also making education more accessible, breaking down traditional barriers of location and cost. Virtual and augmented reality holds the potential to create immersive learning environments, allowing students to engage with complex concepts in ways that were once unimaginable. I already use AI daily, and I can't imagine how it will support us in the future.

As we move forward, education will increasingly focus on cultivating skills vital for the 21st century, such as critical thinking, creativity and emotional intelligence. The notion of lifelong learning will become more relevant as the job market evolves and new opportunities arise. Staying ahead will require continual upskilling and adaptability. Embracing these advancements, education will remain a powerful force for shaping individuals and societies, equipping us to navigate the challenges and opportunities of the future confidently.

So, embrace the learning opportunities and let education be a launchpad of your success. It enhances your ability to tackle problems, advance your career and contribute to youthful ageing.

PATHWAY FIVE

Nutrition for Lifelong Health

'I don't want to be the poster girl for anything in particular, but I don't equate thinness with healthiness, so I don't feel I have to defend having flesh on me. It's, as the French say, everything in moderation – including moderation.'

Nigella Lawson

The Wisdom of Moderation

Nigella Lawson's quote resonates deeply with me. Many people struggle with their weight throughout their lives. I am not a dietitian, nutritionist or food guru, but as a human being, I know that if you deprive me of something, I will crave it immediately! The idea of having moderation, even in moderation, appeals to me because it means I can enjoy some treats along the way.

Two Main Sources of Dietary Advice

The Mediterranean Diet and the Blue Zones
I've already mentioned the enigmatic regions known as the Blue Zones, which have captured the imagination of health enthusiasts and researchers for their inhabitants who defy the odds of ageing. Ikaria, Sardinia and Okinawa are pockets of longevity attributed to lifestyle choices, particularly nutrition. Their diets are mainly Mediterranean, consisting of vegetables, fruits, extra virgin olive oil, wholegrain cereals, legumes, nuts and seeds, fish and seafood, and various herbs and spices. The wisdom of the Blue Zones can guide us to the key ingredients of vitality, longevity and lasting wellbeing.

Plant-Based Eating and The Food Revolution
I recently attended an eight-day online summit, *The Food Revolution*, by John and Ocean Robbins. During the summit, they interviewed various health and food experts. They advocate for a plant-based diet, and I found the science behind their recommendations compelling. Their approach emphasises whole, plant-based foods, which can significantly improve health, reduce the risk of chronic diseases and support environmental sustainability. Following their advice, incorporating more plant-based meals into your diet can lead to numerous health benefits.

Food Availability is Not the Same for Everyone on the Planet
While I offer advice on maintaining a healthy diet, I recognise that adhering to these principles can be challenging in the real world. Many people face obstacles such as food deserts, where access to fresh and nutritious foods is limited, or the overwhelming presence of processed foods that complicate healthy eating. Additionally, varying cultural contexts influence dietary habits and availability. For instance, in areas with limited fresh produce, community-led urban gardening initiatives can provide a vital source of healthy foods. Similarly, adapting traditional recipes to incorporate more wholefoods can help communities adjust to modern dietary challenges. It's essential to consider these factors and approach dietary choices with flexibility and creativity, understanding that even small changes can have a significant impact on overall health and wellbeing.

Cultural Perspectives on Nutrition
Different cultures offer unique insights into nutrition and health. For example, traditional Asian diets often balance flavours and nutrients, reflecting principles of harmony and moderation. In India, Ayurvedic practices guide eating habits based on individual doshas, promoting balance and wellbeing. Similarly, indigenous food practices around the world, such as the use of traditional grains and herbs, contribute to long-term health. The Japanese concept of *hara hachi bu* (eating until 80% full) contributes to health. Exploring these diverse dietary traditions can enrich our understanding of nutrition and offer valuable lessons for maintaining a healthy lifestyle.

Personal Dietary Choices

Expert opinions on nutrition change daily, let alone over the decades. However, a few fundamental principles can support a healthy weight throughout a lifetime.

Food is a Necessity of Life
The first is to see food as essential and life-affirming rather than something to feel guilty about. Food is a perfect way to enjoy family and friends and is indispensable as nutrition.

I love the idea that we are eating the sun. Without the sun, plants would not photosynthesise and capture the energy we need to live and move. The closer you get to eating foods that rely on the sun rather than artificial processes, the healthier and cleaner your diet will be.

I eat meat, though I know many of you don't. The key to a good diet is to get the protein and green vegetables you need. After that, other vegetables and fruits are excellent additions. I can't go a day without bread, especially with butter and Marmite. When I try to ban carbs, I end up binging on them. So, I aim to eat healthily while including a carbohydrate every day. Sinfully, I also have something sweet, often a few squares of chocolate with a cup of tea. When dining out or on vacation, I indulge in dessert because life is too short not to enjoy beautiful food.

Managing Weight and Portions
It's helpful to have a maximum weight in mind. You might exceed it during pregnancy or after a long holiday, but having a number in your head can help you stay on track. I like to think of having ten helpings of food a day. For instance, muesli and milk in the morning count as one helping, while chocolate cheesecake might count as two or three due to its calorie content. My dinner, consisting of protein, vegetables and carbs, counts as three or four, and a coffee with milk counts as one. I tally it up in my head. If I think I went over ten helpings in a day, I might try to balance it out the next day.

There are many ways to track your consumption, such as food diaries or apps. However, I prefer the simplicity of counting to ten. Good nutrition and maintaining a healthy weight contribute to feeling youthful, as you enjoy better health and self-esteem.

*'Every time you eat or drink,
you are either feeding disease or fighting it.'*

Heather Morgan

Tips for Healthy Eating

It's Not About Willpower
A key idea is that a healthy diet doesn't depend on willpower but on good organisation. I am most successful when I take the time to think through where, what and how I will be eating and plan to keep it balanced.

Home-Cooking
A vital family skill is home cooking. It is usually healthier and less calorie-laden than eating out, ordering takeaways or consuming processed meals. Dr Norman Swan recommends a Mediterranean diet, slow-cooking colourful foods, onions and garlic in extra virgin olive oil. His excellent book *So You Want to Live Younger Longer* (Swan, 2022) has lots of advice.

Plan Your Shopping
Never shop when you're hungry. You're much more likely to pile the wrong foods into the trolley. Also, shop around the outer perimeter of

the supermarket, where all the fresh produce is located. Most centre aisles consist of processed, sugar-laden products that are less healthy.

Limit the Calories You Drink
Another trick is to avoid calories in what you drink. Black coffee, tea, mineral water, and plain water are good choices. I like to steep three herbal teabags – green, mint, chamomile or ginger – overnight. While the water is hot, I add a teaspoon of honey sourced from my hive. The next day, it's ready to drink hot, cold or with sparkling water. It's refreshing and subtly sweet. I used to drink many diet sodas, but recent research shows it may be toxic to gut microbiota (Foster, 2024).

Occasional Detoxing or Boosting
Every so often, you might need to cleanse, detox or boost your immune system and health with supplements. For this, it's wise to consult a doctor, nutritionist or dietitian. I have followed this kind of advice at various times and felt the benefits.

It's Never Too Late to Start a Healthy Regime
A relative recently donated blood. After his session, he was advised to see a doctor. He discovered he had high blood pressure and high cholesterol and was pre-diabetic. He was advised to slim down for his own health's sake. He signed up at a slimming group, and within eighteen months, he had dropped four waist sizes. The impact on his health was remarkable. Everything wrong had gone down to within the healthy range. Undoubtedly, according to the old adage, we are what we eat.

Enjoy your food. Appreciate what you have on your plate and the energy it fuels. The healthier we stay throughout life, the more strength and power we will keep in later decades. I am often amazed that my muscle memory for exercise and daily energy levels have stayed consistent from my thirties to my sixties.

PATHWAY SIX

Exercise – The Time Machine to Youthful Energy

'Physical fitness is not only one of the most important keys to a healthy body but also the basis of dynamic and creative intellectual activity.'

John F. Kennedy

Jack LaLanne: The Godfather of Fitness
When Arnold Schwarzenegger admires someone, it's a cue for us all to take notice. Speaking of Jack LaLanne, Schwarzenegger once remarked, 'It doesn't matter where you go, there's a health club, and it all started with Jack LaLanne.' LaLanne, affectionately dubbed the 'Godfather of Fitness,' revolutionised the exercise landscape and left an indelible mark on women's fitness.

Overcoming personal health obstacles in his youth, including poor nutrition and sugar addiction, LaLanne embraced exercise and proper nutrition, igniting a lifelong commitment to health and vitality. His influence transcended gender boundaries, shaping the fitness industry for everyone. He broke barriers and stereotypes by encouraging men and women to engage in strength training and cardiovascular exercise long before it became mainstream. Through his pioneering television program and public appearances, he empowered individuals of all ages and backgrounds to embrace physical activity to enhance their health and wellbeing. His legacy continues to resonate, inspiring people worldwide to lead active, empowered lives.

The Underestimated Key to Wellbeing
The demands of modern life lead us to overlook one of the most potent tools for enhancing health and overall wellbeing: exercise. It plays a crucial role in physical fitness and enhances cognitive acuity and mental health.

Early Beginnings: A Love for Movement
My journey with exercise began early. I vividly recall my fascination with Highland dancers at a fair when I was three. To everyone's surprise, I hopped on stage to join them! From there, my love for movement blossomed through ballet, school sports, hockey, athletics and gymnastics. A few years of dance can improve muscle tone and posture.

Life Skills Through Sport
Besides general fitness, sports provide many life skills. They build perseverance, encourage teamwork, and help you discover your physical capabilities. And it's never too late to start enjoying the benefits of exercise.

The Comprehensive Benefits of Exercise
All exercise improves bone, muscle and core strength. Extension and stretching exercises support flexibility and reduce the risk of injury. Exercise promotes good balance, posture and cardiovascular fitness. Sweating during exercise helps regulate body temperature and releases endorphins, improving mood and reducing stress. The benefits continue for hours after the exertion.

Embracing Fitness: From Gyms to Prenatal Classes
I attended gym classes in my twenties, doing everything from aerobics to weights, and step to stretch classes. Gym classes taught me the importance of correct muscle alignment, laying the foundation for lifelong strength. I attended prenatal classes during pregnancy, understanding the vital role of staying fit and strong. (There will be more on this topic later in the book.)

Competitive Racewalking: A Family Affair
In my thirties, my husband Pierre and I unexpectedly discovered competitive veterans' racewalking. The first time I turned up to 'Fit for Life,' the avenue to my race-walking years, I was pregnant, wearing dangly earrings, a long pink cardigan and leggings. The organising ladies later shared that they took a bet I wouldn't last a fortnight. They were wrong. Facilitated by good coaching and training with peers, Pierre and I earned medals, and I achieved national colours. These walks weren't just physical exertion; some of my most creative and life-transforming ideas were generated during those challenging walks.

The Rewards of Competitive Sports
Competitive sports instil discipline, determination and a sense of accomplishment. Winning events, receiving medals and standing on podiums rewarded our efforts. Since then, when I feel that something in life is too daunting, I think back on those moments and know if I want something badly enough, I'll achieve it. Our family embraced exercise, too. My sister, Helene, took up racewalking, and my brother, Martin, became an international Ironman and ultra-marathon runner, proving that age is no barrier to physical achievement. Honestly, if we could do it, anyone can raise their exercise goals.

Lifelong Activities: From Power Walking to Golf
Currently, I still power walk and have taken up golf. On vacation, my favourite activity is skiing. I know exercise has benefited my body, but it has infinitely enhanced my social life, friendships, sense of self-worth and general happiness. So, whether for your children or yourself, finding a kind of exercise you enjoy is the first step to youthful ageing. It is the most excellent favour you will ever do for yourself.

Incorporating Exercise into Daily Life
Exercise doesn't have to be structured; it can be integrated into daily routines. Taking the stairs instead of the lift or parking further from your destination might seem like small choices, but they make a significant difference over time, contributing to a healthy lifestyle. Even while travelling, keeping an exercise routine is crucial. As we age, maintaining joint health becomes vital. Daily push-ups and squats can significantly improve joint mobility and overall wellbeing. As mentioned before, I often do a routine I call 'the bare minimum' while waiting for the kettle to boil.

Home Routines: Lil's Yogalates
In recent years, I've become less inclined to visit the gym. Despite joining several, my loathness to go out meant I never attended often enough to warrant the cost. So, I created my home exercise routine. Drawing on my past experiences, I put together a forty-minute session I call 'Lil's

Yogalates.' I know ... it sounds like a drink. It includes aerobic exercises, stretches, weights, and routines for upper body, lower body and core strength. I can easily do it at home with inexpensive equipment from a retail outlet. I have a yoga mat, 2- and 3-kg weights, a roller, an elastic exercise band, and two small soccer balls under my hips to take the pressure off my back when lifting my legs for peddling, rotations or leg lifts. It's simple and easy because I don't have to leave the house. I do this routine once or twice a week.

Strengthening Bones and Joints: OsteoStrong
The latest addition to my exercise routine is OsteoStrong, a scientifically-backed method to strengthen bones and joints efficiently. Machines designed for people with osteoarthritis calibrate and build pressure precisely to each person's ability. I have strong bones, but I'm doing it to strengthen my joints. I love it because it's over in under twenty minutes. Its effectiveness, quick sessions and range of recovery facilities make it a highlight of my week. I end the session on a warm hydro massage bed, feeling relaxed and ready to go.

I learned I was above the ninetieth percentile in bone density and strength during my six-month assessment. My hand grips on the left and right are powerful, apparently a sign of longevity. This assessment is not based only on my OsteoStrong visits; I attribute it to lifelong exercise, especially my days of race-walking, which is a weight-bearing exercise.

Embrace the Power of Exercise
Challenging your physical boundaries in a workout builds mental resilience and enhances self-confidence. Regardless of your preferences, incorporating a mix of exercises into your life leads to a well-rounded fitness profile. Exercise offers something for everyone, irrespective of age or ability. Finding activities you enjoy ensures that staying active becomes a lifelong commitment rather than a chore. From childhood sports to embracing fitness in later years, exercise provides physical, mental and emotional benefits.

So, step out, feel the blood pumping and embrace the transformative power of exercise. This pathway to feeling young in later decades cannot be underestimated.

PATHWAY SEVEN

Style, Beauty and Body Care

'Fashions fade, style is eternal.'

Yves Saint Laurent

The Magnetic, Irresistible You

Be magnetic and embrace your uniqueness. Take a cue from Marilyn Monroe and bring out the most confident, authentic version of yourself.

Amy Greene, wife of Marilyn Monroe's personal photographer, Milton Greene, recalled a remarkable incident during a stroll with Marilyn in New York City. Marilyn, enjoying the anonymity of the city, asked Greene a curious question: 'Do you want to see me become her?' Greene agreed and witnessed a subtle transformation. In a magical moment, Marilyn exuded an irresistible charm that caught the attention of passers-by, turning heads and drawing stares as if she had cast a spell.

Greene described this phenomenon as the 'Marilyn Monroe effect,' highlighting Monroe's ability to elevate herself from the ordinary to the extraordinary. She believed her confidence and presence offered a valuable lesson in self-perception, challenging societal norms of self-image. Greene's anecdote reminds us of the transformative power of self-assurance and confidence in a world where many are taught to play down their potential.

This leads me to a favourite quote of mine by Marianne Williamson, one even quoted by Nelson Mandela in his 1994 inaugural speech as president of South Africa:

> 'Our deepest fear is not that we are inadequate. Our deepest fear is that we are powerful beyond measure. It is our light, not our darkness that most frightens us. We ask ourselves, "Who am I to be brilliant, gorgeous, talented, fabulous?" Actually, who are you not to be? You are a child of God. Your playing small does not serve the world. There is nothing enlightened about shrinking so that other people won't feel insecure around you. We are all meant to shine, as children do. We were born to make manifest the glory of God that

is within us. It's not just in some of us; it's in everyone. And as we let our own light shine, we unconsciously give other people permission to do the same. As we are liberated from our own fear, our presence automatically liberates others.'

We are who we are meant to be, and we must stand tall in our identity. Whilst personal style sounds frivolous, it is profoundly serious.

Your Signature Style:
The Path to Youthful Confidence and Energy

Section One: Style and Grace

Yves Saint Laurent's quote at the beginning of the chapter underlines that while fashion is transient, style is enduring. Fashion changes with seasons and trends, but style endures.

Your Inner Radiance, Confidence and Grace
Your signature style reflects your personality, tastes and values. Embracing your style journey is not unthinkingly following trends but crafting a unique image that resonates with your inner self.

An avenue to everlasting youth is developing your style to radiate confidence, capability and individuality in a competitive world. Whether male, female or of another gender identity, style communicates individuality. No matter who you are, how you present yourself to the world can significantly affect how you look, feel and interact with others.

True style is not just about your clothes but also about the aura you exude. Here's how you can cultivate inner radiance:

Embrace a Life Motto
A personal motto can guide your choices and inspire your style. It's a reminder of your values and what you stand for. My favourite inspirational quote is 'Carpe Diem' – to seize the day. These two short words are a reminder that life is short and not to waste it with negativity. My personal motto is 'Audacious leadership and joyful freedom to be – with integrity.' It has sustained me through many challenges in life. It makes me set my shoulders, slap on a smile, and do what is necessary to the best of my ability.

Mantras and Affirmations
Incorporate positive mantras and affirmations into your daily routine to boost your self-confidence and remind you of your worth. One of mine is, 'Don't mess with me. I've birthed children.'

Nurture Your Spirit
Caring for your inner self is as vital as tending to your outward appearance. Engage in practices that nourish your spirit. While many find direction and purpose through their religious beliefs, spirituality can be diverse. Even without following an established religion, you can cultivate a profound connection to the universe and discover your unique life purpose. Embrace authenticity and let your true personality and individuality shine through as you seek deeper connections.

Visualise Success
Visualisation is a powerful tool for achieving your goals. Picture yourself confidently taking the podium, succeeding in your endeavours and radiating grace.

Evolving Your Personal Style

Investing in Your Wardrobe: Quality Over Quantity
Investing doesn't always mean expensive clothes. Basics in clothing can be budget-friendly. Buy reasonably priced solid-coloured separates that fit

well and breathe. Then, spend your well-earned cash on a few luxurious garments. Quality items stand the test of time. Building a versatile and curated wardrobe allows you to mix and match effortlessly while always looking your best.

My mother, Bee, was a genius at looking amazing without breaking the bank, and she passed on many little tricks.

Making Ethical Choices
Ethical issues may concern you. Fashion and beauty encompass a range of concerns, including the exploitation of workers in supply chains, environmental impact and animal cruelty. As a consumer, be more conscious and join those seeking transparency, fair trade practices and cruelty-free products to support evolving ethical standards.

Clothes and Fashion
Embrace clothing trends that align with your style while showcasing your best assets. Dressing in a way that flatters your body type and makes you feel comfortable will boost your confidence.

Experimenting with New Looks
Don't hesitate to step out of your comfort zone and try new looks and styles. Experimentation can lead to exciting discoveries about what suits you best.

Discover Your Colours
Having your colours done by a stylist can help you identify shades that enhance your complexion and make you glow. Wearing your most flattering colours can instantly make you look youthful and vibrant.

Seeking Professional Guidance
Consider consulting a stylist or shopping expert at least once in your life. Their insights can help you make confident fashion choices and elevate your style.

Capture Your Best Moments
To ensure no unflattering photos are circulating, schedule photo shoots at intervals when you're feeling your best. These moments serve as reminders of your radiance and unique style.

The Power of Accessories and Details: Elevating Your Look

Accessories and attention to detail can elevate your style. Here are some tips to consider:

Shoes that Fit
Comfortable, well-fitting shoes enhance your posture and contribute to your overall style and confidence.

Breathable Clothing
Choose clothing made from comfortable and breathable materials. Feeling at ease in your clothes can boost your energy and confidence.

Red Lipstick
A timeless classic, red lipstick can instantly make you feel empowered and put together. It's a symbol of confidence and style. If not red, find your hypnotic colour.

Dress to Impress
Dressing well is not about impressing others but about feeling your best. When you look good, you feel good, and that radiates confidence.

Adding Sparkle: Jewellery by Design
Jewellery is the ultimate accessory. Fortunately, my husband loves jewellery almost more than I do. He loves great design. Over the years, he has bought me exquisite pieces. But jewellery doesn't have to be expensive to be impressive. All you need is a good eye to choose special items that suit your wardrobe and style.

Once, a necklace bought me. I passed a store selling African-inspired merchandise in a Sandton, South Africa, shopping centre. A long, geometric black and white beaded necklace drew me in and forced me to open my purse. Whenever I wear it, it draws comments. Even from passers-by.

Three Tricks to Brighten You Up in Under a Minute
When your hair feels flat, bend over, put your fingers against your scalp and fluff it up. Then reshape it loosely. You'll be surprised how enhanced it is.

When you feel pale and lacking energy just before meeting someone or leaving home, bend over and hang your hands towards the floor. Let the blood drain to your face for a minute or two. Stand up with more colour on your cheeks, smile brightly and feel refreshed. Then step out.

When you're exhausted, sit with your elbows on a table and close your eyes. Place the palms of your hands into your eye sockets. Put gentle pressure on your eyeballs and feel the tiredness receding. Stand up revitalised.

In summary, your style is a dynamic expression of your inner self and preserves an inner youth.

Section Two: Good Health and Self-Care are Sources of Vitality

Facecare: Glowing Skin
Skincare is the cornerstone of maintaining a youthful appearance. Starting a good skincare routine early in life can pay dividends as you age. The power of personalised care is in your hands, as each person's skin is unique and requires a unique approach.

As strongly as we believe our looks are less important than who we are as individuals, first impressions continue to influence judgement by others. Making the best of our natural gifts is worth the effort. We live unfairly in an ageist society. Women especially begin to feel invisible as they mature, and we want to avoid that with every fibre of our being. Is this fair? Hell no. So, what can we do to counteract it?

When I was sixteen, I left home for boarding school, where I learned a lot, not all academically. I learnt to handle myself and my belongings, socialise, avoid trouble (most of the time) and care for others. But what I learned in the communal bathrooms was the most fascinating. My friends used sugar to exfoliate and pasted their faces with bicarbonate of soda to remove impurities. They slathered on body cream before bed, curled their hair overnight with rolled-up stockings and introduced me to a swathe of other interesting and exotic beauty routines. All this activity made me aware of good habits early on. It taught me daily rituals for hygiene and skincare, which are the foundation of radiant skin. I moisturise almost before I open my eyes in the morning.

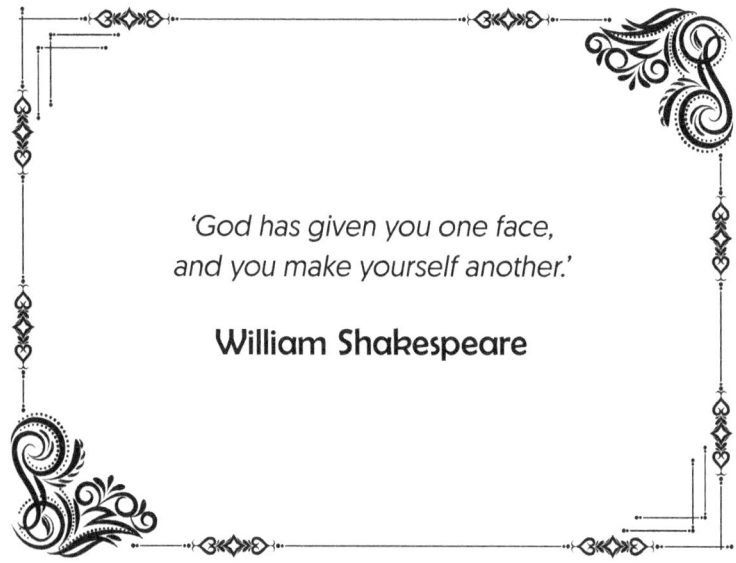

'God has given you one face, and you make yourself another.'

William Shakespeare

Skincare Products
Skincare products range from a few dollars to hundreds, even thousands of dollars a vial.

I can't recommend what to put on your skin because yours is unique, and we all have different budgets and priorities. I can say that being religious about moisturising your skin will be rewarded.

I don't use super expensive creams and lotions. A chemist who formulated skin products once told me in conversation that lanolin and shea butter were excellent allrounders for skin care. I like to vary what I buy because if you use the same thing consistently, your skin gets used to it, and you miss what a different product might add to the overall effect. I also like to vary between oils, serums and lotions, sometimes using two simultaneously. Besides moisturising, regular exfoliation is a step you can't afford to skip, as it helps to keep skin looking fresh and rejuvenated.

During one of my skincare lessons, I learned to treat my entire decolletage as my face. Don't stop your skincare routine at your chin. Extend it to your decolletage. Whatever precious lotion you use on your face should extend down your neck, chest and around to the back of your neck.

Sun Protection
Applying a good sunscreen is more important than moisturising. Because most of my exercise pastimes have been outdoors, I've learned to screen every part of me that will be exposed to the sun, even before I get dressed.

I wear a hat that protects my ears. Skin damage to the scalp and the top of the ears can often lead to severe skin problems, even melanoma, which is prevalent in the southern hemisphere. If I'm outdoors for an extended time, I use SPF 50 and a lotion, including zinc, on my nose and face. Tinted zinc lotions with a creamy consistency are available and work into your skin more efficiently than earlier versions, so you won't look like you're wearing war paint. If the wind is not too strong on the golf course, I put up the umbrella. Some women wear full face masks and gloves on both hands to guard against sun damage, which robs the skin of its youthful appearance.

Home Accessories for the Face
Modern skincare tools like light and vibration-based devices can enhance your routine. A range of accessories are designed to support skin and keep it looking fresh and youthful. However, it's essential to avoid more invasive treatments without professional guidance.

Small appliances use the science of light, sound or vibrations to stimulate cell repair. Battery-run circular brushes stimulate the skin, and even home-use needling tools leave fine pricks on the skin to encourage collagen production in the healing process. I have used the light, sound, vibration and massaging tools, and I like the feel of my skin after use. I would personally avoid doing any needling or controlled wounding at home. In the section on cosmetic procedures, I'll talk more about professional cosmetic skin needling.

More recently, people have started using temperature as a treatment. You can buy a small container to fill with water and freeze. The container is shaped so the ice is rounded to suit the curves on your face. I briefly run the ice over my face once or twice a week, and my skin tingles afterwards.

Make-up Preferences
Your face is a fresh canvas. Quality skincare products and routines mean you can radiate confidence with or without make-up. Whether you use make-up or not is a personal choice. I don't feel fully dressed without my make-up, so I use it daily. People's skin and features differ, and we must seek product advice. Have your skin professionally analysed to ensure you use suitable products to enhance your appearance.

Make-up lessons are excellent for guiding you in applying products to suit your face. You will receive help from having lessons every few years because make-up application changes as you age, and the colours and products require adjustment to continue looking youthful.

Make-up Trends for Everyone
The normalisation of make-up for men and the LGBTQ+ community is a testament to the evolving landscape of self-expression and personal grooming. In recent decades, make-up was relegated to specific groups such as actors, musicians and other public figures. Today, however, the trend is gaining momentum among everyday people, driven by a growing acceptance of beauty products as tools for enhancing appearance and boosting confidence.

One of the most significant gateways into the make-up world has been nail polish. Often seen as a symbol of self-expression, nail polish has helped dismantle traditional gender norms, encouraging more men and LGBTQ+ individuals to explore other cosmetic products. This trend is supported by various new brands explicitly targeting these groups, offering products that cater to their unique skin types and lifestyles. These products, ranging from tinted moisturisers to concealers and bronzers, are designed to be user-friendly, addressing the need for simplicity and efficiency in grooming routines.

Notable public figures and social media personalities are also influencing a more diverse demographic to consider make-up as a universal form of self-care and enhancement rather than a gendered practice. Platforms like TikTok and YouTube have played crucial roles in normalising make-up for everyone, showcasing tutorials and transformations that appeal to a broad audience. This normalisation of make-up broadens the definition of beauty and self-expression. It empowers individuals to feel confident and comfortable in their skin, ultimately promoting a more inclusive approach to personal grooming.

Technology and innovation are poised to revolutionise the beauty industry further. Recent advancements in skincare technology, such as AI-powered routines and cutting-edge dermatological treatments, promise personalised and highly effective solutions for skin health. Meanwhile, virtual try-ons and beauty apps are transforming how we approach personal style, allowing for real-time experimentation with make-up and clothing from the comfort of our homes. These technological innovations enhance our ability to customise our beauty and fashion choices and offer a more interactive and tailored personal style journey.

Maintaining Face and Neck Muscles
The skin is only as firm as the musculature of the face. I heard a radio interview with a foremost Australian actor who said she did facial exercises daily. I was in my fifties, and I'd never heard of them. I downloaded a small book onto my Kindle and read up on facial exercises (Parker, 2014). It made sense that if I was improving the muscle tone in my body, I should do it for my face.

I've been doing exercises consistently for the last twelve years. When you do the exercises, it's essential to hold the area around your eyes gently but firmly so you don't make more wrinkles while exercising. Because I have no idea what my face would be like if I didn't do them, I can't quantify the effect precisely, but I can tell that my face is in a better condition than if I hadn't started the routine.

There are resources to teach facial exercises and facial yoga. Investigate and implement them as a daily habit. I usually do a short set of exercises when waiting for a bath to run, a kettle to boil, or guests to arrive. Any short space of inactivity can be turned into an anti-ageing opportunity.

Teeth: The Gateway to Confidence
A dazzling smile is like an instant age-defying trick. Regular dental care and addressing issues like teeth grinding, which might shorten your teeth over time, are essential for keeping your pearly whites looking great. There are

many tooth whiteners on the market. My preference is for tooth whitening tape. Usually designed to fit the top and bottom teeth, tapes are easy to apply, adhere well to the teeth and are a quick and easy fix.

Dental hygiene is essential. Teeth are one of the quickest things to make you look older or less healthy than you are. Discolouration, cracks or missing teeth need to be addressed. Good hygiene also helps to prevent bad breath, gum disease and general health of the mouth and tongue.

Eyebrows and Lashes
Recent entrants to the beauty market are eyelash and eyebrow serums. Drops initially designed to treat glaucoma were found to promote growth of the eyelashes. On the back of that discovery, a massive eyelash serum industry was created. I started using a serum about a year ago, and my eyelashes are longer and more robust. From having no eyebrows to speak of, they have fully regrown. My optometrist checked the ingredients to ensure they were safe, and she was satisfied. I apply my eyelid cream before painting on the serum so that the serum doesn't go onto my skin. I've been pleased with the outcome.

Glasses and Eyewear
In recent years, I have had to wear glasses more consistently. I noticed that bags appeared under my eyes each time I had my glasses on for a day. It made me aware of the best eyewear and well-fitting glasses. Ensure they're the right fit to avoid the lenses resting or pressing down on the delicate skin around your eyes and upper cheeks. Well-fitted eyewear not only feels better but also looks better.

Hands and Nails
I wish I had started caring for my hands earlier. Hands are a sure sign of age, and it pays to moisturise them regularly.

There is an entire industry dedicated to attractive nails. There are many ways to enhance them and many types of applied nails. You need to research the effects of many of these as they can damage your nails, especially if you remove them in a manner not recommended by manufacturers and nail technologists.

Research shows that collagen can enhance hair and nail growth. I take a dose of liquid collagen each day. My nails are stronger than before and don't split as they used to. This is not to say you should take collagen because it affects each person's gut biology differently, but it's worth investigating.

Feet and Nails
Our nails and feet often go unnoticed, but they deserve some love, too. Regular care, like buffing, manicures, pedicures and foot massages, can make a difference.

Hair Care: Deploy Your Inner Artist
Kickstarting your day with a hair routine is about more than looks; it's about setting a positive tone, expressing your personality and boosting your self-confidence. They're not called good hair days for nothing.

A good hairdresser is your trusted ally. Trying out distinctive styles can boost your confidence and self-image. A hairdresser can advise on which shampoos and conditioners are good for you. There are also straighteners and toners available. I have chosen to colour my hair to cover the greys. Many women embrace their grey hair, and it looks stunning, too. A style that compliments your face and looks fresh and cared for is more youthful than if you don't keep your style up to date.

Multiple hair styling tools are available, so experiment until you find the perfect appliance for your hair. I use a combination of electric curlers and a hairdryer to get my hair in shape each day.

This hair advice extends to men, including their facial hair. Having a shaving routine is a surefire way to boost confidence. Caring for hair in the ears and nostrils is also essential for good grooming.

We all need to find a hair grooming routine that suits our personality and lifestyle so we look and feel our best every day.

Body Care
Caring for your body is just as important as caring for your face. It's a priority for a vibrant, healthy and youthful life. Regular exercise helps maintain muscle tone and supports overall vitality. Our bodies carry us through life's adventures, so caring for them is essential for feeling youthful, inside and out. The earlier you adopt practices and habits to keep and rejuvenate your body, the longer you'll stay strong and mobile.

Body Strength
I have already stressed the importance of exercise for solid muscles and bones. Regular strength training exercises are like sculpting sessions for your muscles. Plus, they help maintain bone density and keep you looking and feeling young. Healthy bones are the foundation of an active life. Maintaining good bone density ensures you stay strong and agile as you age.

Your core strength supports overall stability and confidence. The often-neglected pelvic floor muscles need to be kept strong to avoid prolapse of the internal organs. Kegel exercises are your best friends, and they can be done anytime. I do them while waiting at traffic lights. Paying attention to your core and pelvic floor can make you feel youthful from the inside out.

Body Pampering
Soaps can be dehydrating, so choose a mild, nourishing soap. A full-body moisturiser is necessary to keep skin supple. Regular exfoliation helps maintain a smooth appearance and stimulates blood flow, bringing nutrients to the skin. Dr Norman Swan tells us the skin is our biggest organ, and moisturising can help protect it from harmful bacteria and environmental influences (Swan, 2022).

Find Your Signature Fragrance
Discovering your signature fragrance adds a touch of allure and personal expression to your daily routine. It's a small detail that can make a significant difference. My favourite is Versace *Crytal Noir*.

Comprehensive Beauty Care

Eat and Drink Well for Health
Nutrition and hydration are essential. Foods high in antioxidants found abundantly in colourful fruits and vegetables offer skin protection.

Ample water intake keeps skin moist and vital. It's become fashionable to carry a two-litre bottle around all day. Do whatever you can to stay hydrated. And normal filtered water is the most economical and the best for you and the planet.

Prioritising gut health is essential. Herbs like chamomile and ginseng and adaptogens such as ashwagandha may relieve stress. These lifestyle practices can effectively manage stress-related skin conditions and promote overall wellbeing.

Get Enough Sleep: Rejuvenation in Slumber
Quality sleep is paramount, allowing your body time for regeneration and repair. Prioritise sleep to hit your reset button, leaving you refreshed and ready to tackle each day. Good sleepwear and linen are worth investing in for comfort and wellbeing. Wrap yourself in a bit of luxury and feel your best every night.

Keep Up Your Strength: Physical Maintenance
Maintaining your physical strength is an ongoing commitment. Physiotherapy, myotherapy and massage can be your secret weapons for staying active and vital.

De-stress to Impress
Stress is normal in life. Good stress makes our adrenaline pulse so we can attack a task successfully. But continuous stress can lead to problems. Addressing stress-related conditions involves holistic approaches targeting the mind and body. Experts recommend reducing stress levels.

Practising meditation and mindfulness for just ten minutes daily can significantly alleviate stress. It may not be perfect, but I meditate just before sleep. It helps calm my body and mind, and I generally sleep soundly afterwards.

Similarly, self-massage calms the nerve receptors beneath the skin's surface. I use a great hand-held massager whenever I feel stiff or sore. Regarding aches and pains, I use a TENS machine that emits an electric charge through the muscular area I'm treating. It's invaluable for speeding up healing.

Brain Health: Keeping Your Mind Sharp
Let's not forget about keeping our minds sharp. Challenging activities like puzzles or learning new things are a workout for your intellect. You've already heard about the benefits of education, but daily habits can boost brain health. Crosswords, sudoku, bridge, strategy games and other pursuits keep the grey cells active. Physical activity can also increase the effects of mental workouts.

Section Three: Safeguarding Your Health and Vitality Through Pregnancy

Pregnancy: A Miraculous Phase
Pregnancy is a unique and miraculous phase in a woman's life. It's essential to approach it with a sense of wonder, anticipation and a good dose of practicality.

Information: Knowledge Is Empowerment
Access to reliable information about pregnancy, childbirth and postpartum care empowers you to make informed decisions for your health and your baby's wellbeing. In an era of so many conflicting ideas about care during pregnancy, find the advice that makes sense to you, your culture and your lifestyle.

Preparing for Birth
Explore different birth plans and options to help you feel more prepared and in control of your birthing experience. Attend childbirth education classes and learn about birthing to ease your anxieties and build confidence. Lean on loved ones, family and friends as your support network, both emotionally and practically. Your healthcare professionals are invaluable resources during pregnancy. Establishing trust and open communication with them is essential.

Nourishing Your Body

Diet: Eating for Two
Eating for two is not about eating twice as much (I wished). It is about eating a balanced and nutritious diet to support your and your infant's health. Take heed of the dietary choices recommended by your trusted health professionals. Some expectant mothers may feel nauseous or experience cravings for specific foods. Each person's pregnancy journey is different. It is important to monitor weight to continue feeling healthy. However, some conditions might have you gain more than you'd like. Once you return to your usual self and your baby is settled beyond birth into a routine, you will more easily shed the kilos you might have gained. Focus on how amazing you are to carry and bring a new person into the world. I have never felt more like a queen than when I was pregnant with my son and daughter.

Exercises: Keeping Active and Healthy

Staying active during pregnancy can help manage weight, improve mood and promote better sleep. Safe and beneficial exercises are essential to maintaining vitality. I was fortunate to attend prenatal exercise classes. I learned that, for the most part, you can continue doing what you were used to doing during pregnancy. The strengthening exercises that require the most focus are the abdomen and pelvic floor muscles.

The Stomach Muscle
Understanding how to care for your abdominal muscles and back can help prevent discomfort and promote a smoother pregnancy journey.

Abdominal separation, also called diastasis recti, is common during pregnancy. It occurs when the abdominal muscles part ways under the pressure of a growing baby. Although it usually resolves itself postpartum, it can persist for about one in three individuals, even a year after childbirth. The best cure for separation is preventing the split in the first place.

Signs of abdominal separation may include a visible gap between the abdominal muscles and a sensation of weakened core strength. Preventative measures during pregnancy, such as strengthening core muscles and avoiding activities that strain the abdomen, can help reduce the risk and severity of separation.

Exercising the stomach and oblique muscles with daily crunches can help maintain strength. Get an exercise regime from your advisor and make it your mission to keep your stomach muscles intact.

Post Partum Care of the Abdomen
Avoiding heavy lifting, adopting gentle movement techniques, and performing specific exercises targeting deeper stomach muscles can aid recovery post-birth. Specialist physiotherapy and supportive wearables offer tailored interventions, while surgical options are a last resort for

severe cases. Through awareness, proactive exercise, and attentive postnatal care, individuals can navigate abdominal separation with resilience and determination.

Caring for Skin
It's essential to care for your skin as your body changes. Special oils and Vitamin E creams can help to keep skin supple and may even prevent stretch marks. Start using these when you know you have a baby on the way.

Dress for Comfort and Style
Maternity fashion is much more available now than in my day. Choose comfortable and stylish maternity clothing to boost your confidence and make you feel great throughout your pregnancy. There are fashion houses specialising in maternity wear. There are even garments that 'grow' as you do. Pregnancy is a time to step up your style.

Preparing for the Arrival

Welcoming Your Little One
Preparing for your baby's arrival involves more than just buying baby gear. There are emotional and practical aspects of getting ready for your newborn. It's human nesting. It's also a time to be creative as you design spaces to suit and accommodate your family and personal choices.

Postnatal Care: Beyond Pregnancy
Your journey doesn't end with childbirth. Postnatal care is essential for your recovery and the wellbeing of your baby. Continue strengthening your pelvic floor muscles, supporting postpartum recovery and long-term health. One of the effects of childbirth can be a prolapse of the internal organs. The sooner you strengthen these areas after childbirth, the stronger your body will be for the decades ahead.

Pregnancy is a transformative and beautiful experience. By safeguarding your health and vitality throughout this journey, you're ensuring the wellbeing of your growing baby and nurturing your own physical and emotional vitality. It's a time of profound change, and with the correct information, support and self-care, you can embrace the journey of parenthood with confidence and joy.

Caring for your body during pregnancy can have long-term benefits and help you enjoy a youthful, vibrant body.

Section Four: Managing Menopause to Maintain Strength and Vitality

The second critical time in a woman's life besides pregnancy is menopause. Menopause is a natural biological process marking the end of a woman's reproductive years, typically occurring between ages forty-five and fifty-five. It involves significant hormonal changes, particularly a decline in oestrogen and progesterone levels, which can lead to various symptoms and challenges. I was fortunate to weather menopause well without extreme symptoms. I attribute it to being fit, exercising regularly and maintaining a healthy diet. Managing menopause effectively to maintain strength and vitality requires a multifaceted approach tailored to each individual's unique experience and needs.

Understanding the Variability of Menopause
Every woman's experience with menopause is different. Some may go through this transition with minimal discomfort, while others might face more severe symptoms such as hot flashes, night sweats, mood swings, sleep disturbances and weight gain. The variability in symptoms means that there is no one-size-fits-all solution for managing menopause.

Hormonal Changes and Management
The hormonal fluctuations during menopause are at the core of many symptoms. Oestrogen and progesterone are necessary for various bodily functions, including bone density, cardiovascular health and mood regulation. As these hormone levels drop, women may experience:

- Bone density loss: increased risk of osteoporosis
- Cardiovascular changes: elevated risk of heart disease
- Mood swings and cognitive changes: potential for anxiety, depression and memory issues.

Managing these changes often involves hormone replacement therapy (HRT), which can help alleviate symptoms by replenishing oestrogen and progesterone levels. However, HRT is not suitable for everyone and carries potential risks, such as increased chances of blood clots and certain cancers. Consult a medical professional to weigh the benefits and risks and to determine the most appropriate treatment plan.

Lifestyle and Non-Hormonal Approaches
In addition to or instead of HRT, various lifestyle changes and non-hormonal therapies can help maintain strength and vitality during menopause:

- Nutrition: a balanced diet rich in calcium, vitamin D and phytoestrogens (found in soya products) supports bone health and may mitigate some symptoms
- Exercise: regular physical activity, including weight-bearing exercises, can help maintain bone density, improve cardiovascular health and boost mood and energy levels
- Stress management: yoga, meditation and mindfulness can reduce stress and improve mental wellbeing
- Sleep hygiene: establishing a regular sleep routine and creating a restful environment can alleviate sleep disturbances.

Medical Advice and Personalised Care
Consulting with healthcare providers is crucial in developing a comprehensive menopausal management plan. Medical professionals can offer personalised advice based on individual health profiles, symptom severity and risk factors. They may recommend a combination of HRT, lifestyle adjustments and other treatments like antidepressants or medications for osteoporosis.

In conclusion, managing menopause to maintain strength and vitality involves a personalised approach considering the wide range of experiences and symptoms women may face. By addressing hormonal changes through professional medical advice and adopting supportive lifestyle habits, women can navigate this transition with resilience and wellbeing.

Section Five: Cosmetic Procedures: Enhancing Your Natural Beauty

Everyone is Unique
Just as make-up and skincare have become normalised for all genders, so too have cosmetic procedures. Everyone is unique, and I am not a qualified professional. In this chapter, I share my personal experiences to offer some insights. It's important to remember that what works for one person may not work for another. This individuality is crucial when considering any changes to your appearance or health.

Precautions and Risks
When it comes to cosmetic procedures, it's essential to be fully aware of the risks involved. Procedures, especially the more invasive ones, come with potential complications. It's crucial to do thorough research and consult with qualified professionals. Many experts warn that the decision to undergo a cosmetic procedure should never be taken lightly.

Personal Viewpoint

I have always believed in enhancing one's natural features rather than completely altering them. This belief has guided my decisions regarding personal care and any cosmetic procedures I have undergone. My journey has been of careful consideration and a desire to maintain my authenticity.

Balanced Perspective

It's vital to approach cosmetic changes from a balanced perspective. Decisions should not stem from insecurity but rather from a place of self-enhancement. Embracing one's unique features while considering subtle enhancements can lead to the best outcomes. Nothing should be done due to insecurity but more from a balanced perspective, especially when procedures become more invasive.

Cosmetic Procedures: From Least to Most Invasive

Skin Treatments

Cosmetic skin treatments offer various benefits to keep the skin radiant and youthful. Laser therapy targets deeper skin layers to rejuvenate and repair, reducing wrinkles and scars. Light therapies like IPL and LED treatments address age spots and rosacea. Sound therapy uses ultrasound to stimulate collagen production and lift sagging areas.

Microneedling is a popular method that stimulates collagen production and improves skin texture by creating micro-injuries on the skin's surface. There are several kinds of skin needling or controlled wounding techniques. I have used these treatments for years. A decade ago, they were pretty painful, but improvements in the machines and the skin-numbing methods have made them much easier and more pleasant. The effects last for quite a few months. I go once a year for a series of three treatments. The idea is that the skin's biological action to heal the micro-wounds triggers collagen production. But do your research before you embark on any of these treatments.

Eye Surgery
Eye surgeries can improve vision and enhance aesthetic appearance. LASIK corrects refractive errors, while procedures like eyelid lifts or blepharoplasty address sagging eyelids and under-eye bags, providing a more youthful look. In my early fifties, I had a lens replacement in one eye to improve my close vision. This was essentially a cataract operation. It took my brain a couple of months to adapt to having one eye focused on what was close and the other on distance. It worked very well for about ten years, and I have only recently had to revert to glasses for reading.

Aesthetic Enhancements
Non-surgical aesthetic enhancements, such as Botox injections and dermal fillers, reduce wrinkles and fine lines. These treatments can boost self-confidence and body image without invasive surgery.

Facelift: Restoring Youthful Contours
A surgical facelift, or rhytidectomy, tightens facial muscles and removes excess skin to restore a youthful appearance. While it offers significant results, it involves more downtime and risks than non-surgical treatments.

Breast Surgery: Personal Choices
Breast augmentation or reduction surgeries reshape the breasts to enhance body contours and address personal comfort. These procedures require careful consideration due to potential complications and recovery time. Be aware that if you have implants, they will need to be removed or replaced at some point meaning more than one surgery.

Reshaping Your Image: Personal Empowerment
For many individuals, cosmetic procedures offer a sense of personal empowerment and increased self-esteem. Achieving desired physical changes can boost confidence and contribute to a positive self-image, ultimately improving overall wellbeing.

Balancing Expectations and Realities
Approach cosmetic procedures with realistic expectations. While these treatments can provide noticeable improvements, they may not necessarily achieve perfection or resolve deeper emotional or psychological issues. Communicating openly with qualified medical professionals and seeking procedures for the right reasons is essential, focusing on enhancing self-confidence rather than conforming to external ideals.

Understanding Risks and Recovery
Every medical procedure carries inherent risks, and cosmetic treatments are no exception. Potential complications, such as infection, scarring or adverse reactions, should be thoroughly discussed with a qualified healthcare provider. Additionally, understanding the recovery process and post-operative care is essential to achieving the best results and minimising discomfort.

Each cosmetic procedure, from non-invasive treatments to surgeries, offers unique benefits and considerations. It's essential to approach these decisions with realistic expectations and thorough research, consulting with qualified professionals to ensure the best outcomes for your health and appearance.

Body care isn't just about looking young; it's about feeling youthful and vibrant from the inside out. So, remember, whether you prioritise health or enhance your appearance, it's all part of a comprehensive wellbeing approach that nurtures your body, mind and spirit.

Section Six: Avoid Smoking, Alcohol and Recreational Drugs

Alright, let's have a little chat. I'm about to sound like your overly cautious great-aunt. I know, I know – the idea of not smoking, steering clear of recreational drugs and keeping your alcohol intake in check might make me seem like a bit of a killjoy. But stick with me here! While it may sound like conventional advice, there are compelling reasons to consider these habits. So, as you roll your eyes, take a moment to see how changes can significantly enhance your health and wellbeing.

Smoking
Don't let your beauty go up in smoke.

The best way to stop smoking or vaping is never to start. Unfortunately, I was a smoker for eight years, from seventeen to twenty-five. Luckily, I decided to give it up. It wasn't easy, and I needed professional support to do it.

Smoking is hazardous to health. Air is the breath of life. Spending days or years coughing, battling to breathe, and even carting oxygen around with you are not attractive scenarios. I started because I thought it would help me lose weight. It didn't, and it came with many negatives.

A positive is that your lungs start to heal the moment you give up. So even if you've smoked for a long time and think giving up won't make a difference, it does. Give up now. Do yourself one of the biggest favours of your life.

Alcohol and Drugs
In our pursuit of youth, vitality and overall wellbeing, we need to address a topic that often goes unspoken: the use and misuse of alcohol and recreational drugs. While moderation in life's pleasures is key, overindulgence in substances can adversely affect your physical and financial health. Let's explore how making informed choices can contribute to your overall wellbeing.

I have never taken recreational drugs, and I passionately believe the best thing to do is never start. That said, we know that drugs flood our society. All we can do is try to protect ourselves and our children from the scourge. Understand that drug lords across the globe have you and your children in their sights. And there is a proliferation of targeted drug crime in both urban and country areas in Australia. The extent and depth of drug crime across the globe are nothing short of terrifying.

Learning to Drink in Moderation

One of the first steps in safeguarding youth, vitality and financial health is learning the art of moderation in alcohol consumption. When enjoyed in moderation, alcohol can be a part of social gatherings and celebrations without posing significant risks. However, the key lies in understanding your limits and practising self-control.

You Don't Need Alcohol

It's essential to recognise that you don't need alcohol to have a fun time. Society often portrays alcohol as a social lubricant, but it's not a prerequisite for enjoying life's moments. Many people find that they can have more authentic and memorable experiences when they are fully present rather than relying on alcohol as a crutch. I am delighted that there is a growing trend among young people to abstain from alcohol.

Opting for Virgin Drinks

I gave up alcohol twelve years ago, and it is one of the best life decisions I ever made. At first, I missed the sense of occasion you get when you have a drink in your hand. However, that was overcome at a landmark dinner with friends, where we, the non-drinkers, decided we would never again have an ordinary glass. Any drink in a beautiful glass feels special. I also challenge cocktail makers to make my virgin drinks the sexiest ones in the room. I've had drinks that looked like a tropical holiday in a glass. A virgin mojito is a perfect way to sparkle up an evening. Moreover – I never have a hangover.

The Financial Impact of Alcohol and Recreational Drug Use

Beyond the physical consequences, the financial health of individuals can be severely affected by excessive alcohol and drug use. The costs associated with purchasing alcohol and recreational drugs, as well as potential legal consequences and healthcare expenses, can add up significantly over time.

Safeguarding your financial wellbeing means making conscious choices about distributing your resources. By refraining from excessive spending on alcohol and recreational drugs, you free up resources for more meaningful and enriching experiences in life.

While the allure of alcohol and recreational drugs may be enticing, it's essential to approach them with caution and mindfulness. Learning to drink in moderation, recognising that you don't need alcohol to enjoy life, and opting for alcohol-free alternatives, can help you safeguard your youth, vitality and financial health. By making informed choices in this area, you can prioritise your overall wellbeing and lead a fulfilling and financially responsible life.

Quick Action Rather Than Regrets: Health Proactivity

Being proactive is vital when it comes to health. Addressing concerns as soon as they arise, whether they're minor or not, can prevent more significant issues down the road.

Schedule regular check-ups. Catching health issues early means fewer regrets. It's all about staying one step ahead. Do whatever you can to sustain your health.

This entire chapter on health and beauty links with all the other pathways in the book, which collectively impact feeling stronger, younger, healthier and happier to face life with a youthful edge.

PATHWAY EIGHT

Self-Care and Self-Protection

'You are your last line of defence in safety. It boils down to you.'

Kina Repp

Be Aware, Prepare with Care and Stay Safe Out There

It is a regrettable reality that humans are susceptible to misfortune, ill health, injury and mishaps. Traumatic events in life can and do harm both mental and physical health. Fortunately, our modern world supports us in recovering from or optimising recovery from these events. This said, there are many situations we can avoid if we are adequately prepared. This section is dedicated to helping you remain vigilant and knowledgeable about keeping yourself safe and your body as functional and intact as possible.

It helps if you embrace the fact that you are responsible for your safety. I know this statement is controversial. People say it's not a woman's role to keep herself safe; it's society's. If I felt we could rely on that mantra, I'd say go ahead, go where you want, with whom you want, dressed as you want for as long as you want. But sadly, life is not that simple. So, to be responsible, we need to be concerned about our safety. The same advice applies to all genders and to all young people who are venturing into the world.

Looking after your safety, security and physical and mental health cannot be overstated in a world filled with challenges and opportunities. This pathway highlights vigilance, proactive measures and informed choices in ensuring your safety. Special laws introduced over time are evidence of growing awareness around personal safety.

Brodie's Law
Brodie's law, Victoria's anti-bullying legislation, began in June 2011 and made severe bullying a crime punishable by up to 10 years in jail. Brodie's Law was introduced after the tragic suicide of a young woman, Brodie Panlock, who was subjected to relentless bullying in her workplace.

Statistics of domestic, social and criminal violence to citizens, especially women, show a necessity to develop strategies to keep yourself as safe as possible.

Online bullying is on the increase, and young people, in particular, are the targets, with lasting harmful effects.

To have youth, good looks and health, safeguarding your body is essential. There is no point in spending time and money on your appearance if you don't also keep yourself as safe as possible.

Feeling Safe and Secure

Taking Up Space
Never shrink yourself to accommodate others; take up all the space you need to express your authentic self. People will take you more seriously if you stand tall, walk briskly and address them confidently. Evidence shows you're less likely to be attacked if you walk confidently with purpose.

Body Language
Learn to read body language to anticipate or predict others' intentions and actions. A podcast I once heard discussed how women unconsciously and subtly allow men to dominate social situations. Valuable advice from the podcast is to sit or stand straight and avoid inclining your head when listening or talking. Maintaining direct eye contact conveys a sense of equality. However, it's essential to understand and respect cultural norms that may vary. Regardless of background, never allow yourself to be denigrated, disrespected, trivialised or taken advantage of.

Collecting Information
Educate yourself about self-care and protection. Stay informed about safety practices, security measures and wellbeing strategies. Equip yourself with the information needed to make wise decisions.

Having Backup
Build a support system and create backup strategies. Feeling safe goes beyond physical security; it includes mental and emotional security. Build

a staunch support system of friends and family to aid and comfort you in times of need. Ensure you have contact numbers in a small notebook or on your phone to reach them or the relevant emergency services.

Backup extends to emergency preparedness. Always plan for unexpected situations, such as having some cash and essential phone applications to help you in uncomfortable circumstances.

Respecting Yourself and Your Space
Know your rights and assert boundaries to protect yourself from mistreatment or exploitation. Many young people are manipulated and blackmailed into enduring untenable conditions. The more you're aware of patterns of manipulation, the more confident you'll be in advocating for your wellbeing and personal space. It's crucial to have someone to talk to. In an abusive situation, it's essential to access the necessary care and support as quickly as possible. If family and friends aren't available, the following line of defence is organisations that support victims of abuse.

Zero Tolerance
Never accept ill-treatment or disrespect, whether in personal relationships or professional environments. Uphold your self-worth and set up boundaries that demand equivalence in relationships. If you experience issues, use the available channels to make them known. No-one becomes more respected by being silent about their mistreatment.

Securing Valuables and Identity
Protect your valuables and personal identity by investing in secure storage and document management. Safeguarding your financial and personal information is crucial. If your identity is stolen, it takes months, if not years, to get back on track, and sometimes the losses are permanent.

Vigilance
Your first line of defence is vigilance. Be watchful and aware of potential threats in your surroundings, personal boundaries, and online presence.

Staying vigilant can prevent accidents and attacks and protect your privacy. When approaching your car, a minimum strategy is to have your car key in your hand, which is used for defence. Invest in a personal alarm that emits a loud, piercing sound to frighten off any potential attacker.

Dating in the Modern World
Modern dating can be both exciting and challenging. Trust your instincts when meeting new people and show clear boundaries. Ensure your safety by letting someone know your whereabouts when going on dates. Meet for the first time in a public place.

Be Aware of Drink Spiking
Drink spiking is a dangerous act where an individual deliberately adds alcohol or drugs to another person's drink without their knowledge. This can lead to severe consequences such as loss of consciousness, memory lapses and vulnerability to crimes such as theft or assault. To avoid drink spiking, it is essential never to leave drinks unattended, only accept beverages from trusted individuals, and avoid sharing or swapping drinks. Utilising drink covers and staying alert in social settings can also reduce the risk of drink spiking, ensuring personal safety.

Navigating the Digital Landscape
Safeguarding your online identity in today's digital age is paramount. Use privacy settings, avoid oversharing personal information, and be cautious about accepting friend requests from unknown individuals. Cybersecurity is essential for maintaining digital safety. Unfortunately, stories of catfishing are common, and many people have lost their life savings to unscrupulous operators.

Care Around Photographs
Share your photographs with caution. They are a window into your life. Exercise discretion when sharing images online to ensure they do not compromise privacy and security. Think twice before posting location-specific photos. It is imperative to safeguard your intimate images. It

may sound prudish, but the misuse of personal photographs to shame or blackmail is widespread and highly damaging. This is especially so for teens who may not anticipate the consequences of sharing intimate photos.

Knowing When to Move
Adapting to circumstances in life can present unexpected challenges. Recognise when situations require you to change for your safety and wellbeing. Trust your instincts and take the necessary action. This might mean moving out of a venue, a home, a school, a neighbourhood, a state or even a country. Much easier said than done, I know from one who has experienced it. But if you have the resources and the ability to do it, go ahead. You will never regret it.

Empowerment Through Skills and Taking Care
Learn to drive. It is a practical addition to your self-care, independence and safety. Take self-defence classes. Knowing what to do if you are under attack can save you and others from harm and may even save your life.

Keep sharp objects safe. Ensure knives are always packed with the sharp edge facing down in drawers; hang them on a magnetic holder or keep them in a knife block on your bench. A friend of mine did enormous damage to her hand when she reached into a drawer in a hurry to get something.

Keep an emergency kit in your home and car, including first aid supplies, water, non-perishable food, and essential medications. Practise emergency drills for fire, natural disasters or home intrusions. Knowing what to do can save precious time during an actual emergency.

Safeguarding your protection is a lifelong commitment to your safety, security and overall health. By embracing vigilance, respecting your boundaries and staying informed, you empower yourself to navigate life's challenges confidently and resiliently. Remember that your wellbeing is precious; prioritising it ensures you lead a fulfilling and flourishing life.

Ten Strategies for Keeping Safe

1. Be aware of your surroundings: stay focused in public spaces, minimise distractions like phone use and headphones, and regularly scan your surroundings.
2. IF YOU SEE SOMETHING, SAY SOMETHING: trust your instincts and immediately report any suspicious activity or items to the proper authorities.
3. Know about threats: report any suspicious packages or unattended items to the police immediately.
4. Walk with purpose: walk confidently with your head up to deter potential predators. Project an air of preparedness and focus.
5. Always lock doors: lock your car, especially when refuelling at petrol stations and lock the door of your hotel or other holiday accommodation.
6. Leave space when driving: keep enough space between your vehicle and others for a quick escape.
7. Face entrances: position yourself to have a clear view of doors and entrances, giving you an advantage in spotting potential threats.
8. Self-defence: consider investing in self-defence classes to protect yourself in dangerous situations.
9. Know your limits: understand the human response to danger and mentally prepare to react quickly and effectively. Practise self-defence techniques and be ready to defend yourself if needed.
10. Stay vigilant together: public safety is a collective effort. By staying vigilant and looking out for each other, we can enhance our security and protect our communities, neighbourhoods or even states or countries. It's easier said than done, but if you can do it, you won't regret it.

PATHWAY NINE

Finding Purpose and Energy in Work

'Your work will fill a large part of your life, and the only way to be truly satisfied is to do what you believe is great work. And the only way to do great work is to love what you do.'

Steve Jobs

Work is more than just a means to make a living; it's a fundamental aspect of human life. It can provide you with a profound sense of purpose.

Work: A Source of Purpose

Many people feel restricted or trapped in their work roles. They think they have no power to change how things run. But engaging in meaningful work keeps your mind sharp and your spirit youthful. Loving what you do is the ultimate source of motivation. It doesn't feel like a chore when you're passionate about your job. It gives you a reason to get out of bed every morning.

Finding your niche in the workplace requires defining what you want to achieve personally and having strategic goals to achieve that. A simple work mantra is to work hard, work smart and work ethically. In the ever-changing work environment, some factors can enhance your status and area of influence.

Work Ethic
A strong work ethic is the foundation of achievement. It instils discipline, responsibility and perseverance, contributing to an accomplished life. But don't miss out on essential breaks. Some people proudly say they never take a day off sick leave. Balance your work against your health.

Accomplishing Career Goals
Accomplishments at work can boost your self-confidence. Each success contributes to a positive self-image. Setting and working towards ambitious goals is invigorating and can drive you to achieve more than you thought possible.

Professionalism
Maintaining an elevated level of professionalism in your work not only earns the respect of your peers and superiors but also enhances your self-esteem and confidence. Being reliable and accountable makes you a worthy employee.

Time Awareness
An essential related skill is time management. You can make the best of your time if you plan and prioritise tasks. Punctuality is a sign of respect for your work and the people you work with. Managing your time efficiently reduces stress and boosts your productivity and vitality. Be seven minutes early for everything.

Be a Self-Starter
Most workplaces appreciate people who take the initiative. It pays to be proactive and add value to the organisation. This might involve finding new ways to solve problems, adding to the industry's offerings, streamlining and improving what is already in place or taking on more responsibility.

Good Communication Skills
Effective communication skills will augment your initiative. Both initiative and communication help you form the necessary relationships with peers and leadership who can implement the changes you'd like to see. Cultivate strong professional relationships with colleagues, mentors and stakeholders to gain support and advance your career opportunities.

Emotional Intelligence
If you use emotional intelligence in your dealings, your workplace will benefit. EQ helps you understand and effectively manage your and others' emotions. Understanding yourself and others improves teamwork to achieve common goals. Being a team player will enhance your mobility within an organisation.

Be a Change Agent
Life has few certainties, but we know that things are constantly changing. To succeed at work, being up-to-date with industry trends is essential. This might mean getting new skills to enhance your ability and pursuing professional development to remain competitive. Rather than fear change, embrace it and become the one who proves flexible, handles emerging situations and makes your organisation a dynamic trendsetter.

Work is Not Limited to a Career
Not everyone's work is in an office. And not all work is to earn a salary. Whether you are a stay-at-home parent or a go-out-and-work one, it's essential to derive value from what you do. Loving what you do is the ultimate source of motivation and vitality.

Whether pursuing a career, a hobby or a personal passion, work can be a wellspring of fulfilment and a source of enduring vitality.

As we live longer, the future of work is becoming more exciting for everyone. Traditional career paths are giving way to the gig economy, where short-term and flexible jobs are becoming more common. In this setup, people can choose their hours and pick projects that match their interests and skills. This shift supports work-life integration, which means blending work with personal life to enhance overall happiness. Instead of separating work and individual activities, this approach allows them to complement each other, leading to a more balanced and fulfilling lifestyle.

In this changing work environment, personal branding and ongoing career development are more important than ever. With the rise of digital platforms, building a strong personal brand helps people stand out and align their work with what they care about. Continual learning and professional growth are key to staying satisfied and adaptable in today's world. By embracing these ideas, individuals can make the most of their longer lives, turning each stage into a new chance for growth, fulfilment and meaningful work.

You may wonder why work is related to youth. But once again, it contributes to financial wellbeing and your ability to afford food, exercise and other benefits that make you feel young and vibrant.

If we return to the Blue Zones, the people live by a concept called Ikigai. It means you know your core and your value. You have a purpose, a mission and meaning in life. You count and you're needed.

I can't think of anything more wonderful to bolster self-esteem and add vibrance to your life than Ikigai.

PATHWAY TEN

Unlocking Creativity for Vitality

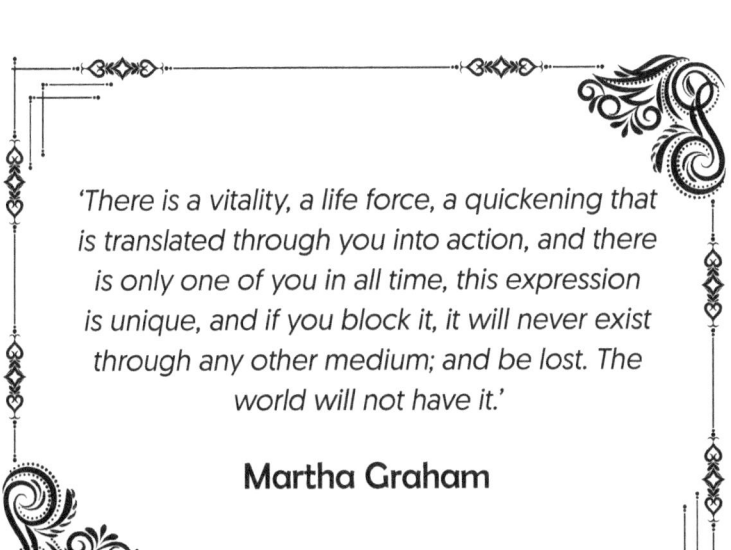

'There is a vitality, a life force, a quickening that is translated through you into action, and there is only one of you in all time, this expression is unique, and if you block it, it will never exist through any other medium; and be lost. The world will not have it.'

Martha Graham

Nurturing Your Creative Spirit

Creativity is not reserved for a select few – it's a quality everyone can tap into. It's about imagining, innovating and expressing our unique selves. Aside from being just a hobby, creativity is vital in enriching our lives. While I may not adhere to traditional religious beliefs, I view creativity as a meaningful gift to humanity.

Edith Wharton offered wise advice on spreading light: be the candle or the mirror reflecting it. By embracing your creative abilities, you illuminate your path and support the creative expressions of those around you.

Embrace Creativity Through Hobbies

Throughout my life, I've explored various activities such as crochet, sewing, floristry, aromatherapy, puppetry and writing. After a few years away from teaching to study fashion design and management, I found these skills surprisingly interconnected. When I took on the Director of Early Learning role, I used these diverse talents in ways I hadn't anticipated, from sewing costumes for school events to arranging flowers and storytelling with puppets.

Digital Platforms are Your Ateliers

I regularly fall into the creative flow with modern tools like Canva, Audacity, Chat GPT, Grammarly, Photoshop and more. I've found these modern applications to be incredibly transformative. I've used them to write books, craft articles and create courses while also learning a lot about design. I often fall down a rabbit hole and lose track of time as I immerse myself in the process. I emerge hours later with hollow eyes and unexpected, satisfying results.

Everyone Can be a Producer

This personal experience highlights a broader truth: everyone can become a creator in today's digital landscape. The available tools make expressing ideas, sharing knowledge and producing content easier. So, be a producer, videographer, writer, musician, podcaster or whatever interests you.

Embracing digital upskilling allows you to leverage these applications, unlocking new ways to bring your creative visions to life. By continually learning and experimenting, you can discover new possibilities, enhance your skills and enjoy seeing your ideas come to fruition.

Preserving Culture Through Creativity
Cultural expression through creativity enriches our lives and helps preserve and pass on traditions to future generations. We celebrate and explore diverse customs by engaging in creative projects, ensuring our cultural heritage remains vibrant and relevant. This process allows us to share our values and stories with our children, preserving a deeper connection to their roots. Additionally, creativity can drive social change by addressing pressing issues and inspiring progress. Through art, literature and other forms of expression, you can raise awareness, challenge norms and contribute to a more thoughtful and progressive society, leaving a meaningful legacy for those who follow.

Whether you engage in dance, arts and crafts, music, technology or any other creative pursuit, these activities can offer enrichment and energy. Creativity is a path to genuine self-expression. Don't hesitate to explore new interests and step outside your comfort zone. Doing so can lead to personal growth, new opportunities and connections with others who share your creative passions.

PATHWAY ELEVEN

Fun and Relaxation

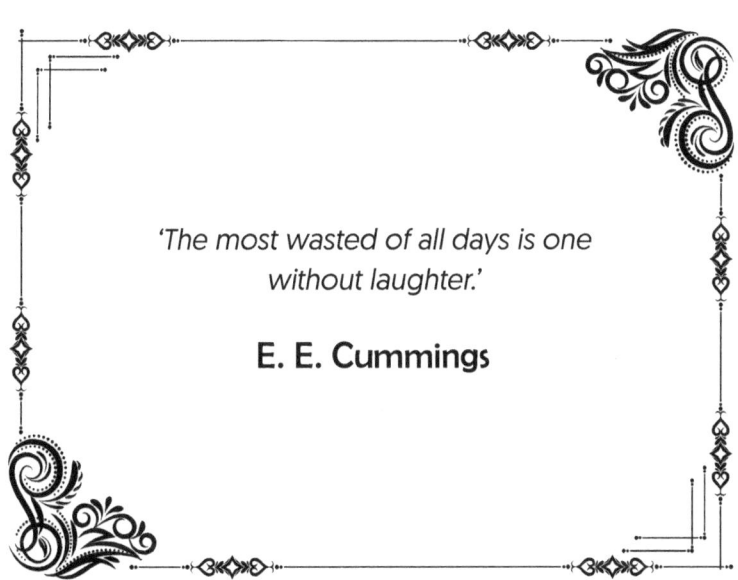

'The most wasted of all days is one without laughter.'

E. E. Cummings

In the hustle and bustle of life, it's easy to become trapped in responsibilities and obligations. Amid life's demands and stresses, we need respite and carefree enjoyment. Carving out time for leisure boosts energy and wellbeing. Plan fun events and keep a diary. So many great memories and experiences are forgotten.

Holidays are more than a break from work; they allow you to pause, rejuvenate and explore the world. Whether basking on a sun-soaked beach or exploring new cultures, holidays offer a chance to create cherished memories. Having fun and engaging in enjoyable activities directly impacts your mental wellbeing. It can alleviate symptoms of anxiety and depression, enhance creativity and improve overall mood.

Parties and celebrations affirm the vibrancy of life. Gathering with friends and loved ones, sharing laughter and stories and indulging in treats contribute to a sense of joy and belonging. Laughter has been shown to decrease stress hormones and boost the immune system (Holden, 1998). Fun and frivolity release endorphins that reduce tension and promote relaxation.

Throughout our lives, we have loved hosting themed parties. These events have provided so many beautiful memories, and we learnt something new about our friends every time they arrived at the door, bearing smiles and wine. One of our favourites was Pierre's most recent decade birthday, with the help of the staff of Fawlty Towers on hand to entertain our guests. Basil told everyone to go home because it was too early.

Downtime is not laziness; it's an essential part of self-care. Whether curled up with an enjoyable book, strolling through a park, or doing nothing, downtime recharges your spirit. Watching a movie, attending a concert or going on a hike helps you escape from daily worries.

Social activities strengthen bonds with friends and family. Shared experiences create lasting memories and reinforce a sense of connection and belonging.

Contrary to what some may believe, fun and leisure enhance productivity. Regular breaks and enjoyable activities recharge your mind, making you more focused and efficient when you return to your tasks.

Fun and leisure infuse vitality into our existence and are essential components of wellbeing. By embracing holidays, celebrations, downtime and the simple joy of having fun, we nurture our spirits, cultivate stronger connections and find balance. So, let loose, embrace the laughter and savour the joy that each moment offers (Holden, 1998).

PATHWAY TWELVE

Financial Literacy for a Secure Future

'Financial freedom is freedom from fear.'

Robert Kiyosaki

The Ant and the Grasshopper
> In a field one summer's day, a Grasshopper was hopping about, chirping and singing to its heart's content. An Ant passed by, bearing with great toil an ear of corn he was taking to the nest.
>
> 'Why not come and chat with me,' said the Grasshopper, 'instead of toiling and moiling in that way?'
>
> 'I am helping to lay up food for the winter,' said the Ant, 'and recommend you do the same.'
>
> 'Why bother about winter?' said the Grasshopper; 'We have plenty of food at present.' But the Ant went on its way and continued its toil.
>
> When the winter came, the Grasshopper had no food and found itself dying of hunger. Then, it saw the ants distributing corn and grain from the stores they had collected in the summer. Then the Grasshopper knew: it is best to prepare for days of need.
>
> Aesop (Short Stories, 2024)

Financial health is essential in our youthfulness, vitality and wellbeing quest. Our choices with our finances can significantly change our stress levels, sense of security and ability to care for ourselves and our loved ones. Financial literacy and wise decisions cannot be underestimated. They start with financial discipline, saving and early implementation of investment strategies. Healthy finances reduce stress and offer better control over your future.

Control Over Your Assets: Empowerment Through Ownership
Having control over your assets means being the custodian of your financial destiny. By taking ownership of your financial affairs and assets,

you gain independence and shape your financial future. Developing healthy spending habits can improve your financial wellbeing. Track expenses, create a budget and prioritise needs over wants. Regularly review your financial situation and set realistic spending limits.

Being Careful with Money: The Foundation of Financial Health
Financial health, comfort and freedom take more than being careful with your money. Beyond budgeting, tracking expenses and living within your means, everyone can access advice on building investments and compounding the effects of savings.

Earning: Building a Strong Financial Foundation
Out of the starting blocks earning a sustainable income is a fundamental aspect of financial health. Investing in your education and acquiring valuable skills increases your earning potential. Additionally, seeking career advancement opportunities and exploring diverse income streams can further bolster your financial stability.

Saving: The Path to Financial Freedom
Saving is the first step towards financial security. Regularly setting aside some of your income allows you to build an emergency fund. A robust savings plan provides peace of mind and enables you to weather unexpected financial challenges.

Being Prepared and Alert
Online banking tools can significantly simplify managing your finances, but protecting your financial information is crucial. Use strong, unique passwords, enable two-factor authentication, and stay alert to phishing scams and other online threats. Plan for potential costs like healthcare expenses in retirement. Understand your health insurance coverage, estimate future medical needs, and set aside funds for these costs to protect your savings. Insurance is essential for managing risk. Ensure you have adequate health, life and property insurance to protect against unexpected events. This coverage is a vital part of a solid financial plan.

Navigating Taxes and Superannuation: Securing Your Future
Understanding the tax system and making informed decisions about superannuation retirement savings are necessary for long-term financial health. By optimising your tax strategies and actively managing your superannuation, you can ensure financial security in your retirement years. Stay informed about updates, explore additional savings options and adjust your plan to provide economic security in your later years. Women, in particular, need to be aware of this.

Females and Finances
Across the globe, women often face lower wages, part-time employment and career interruptions due to caregiving responsibilities, which can significantly impact their financial security. Awareness and proactive steps can help mitigate these challenges.

Firstly, understand the importance of negotiating fair pay and seeking opportunities for career progression. Women can benefit from seeking organisational roles with enhanced parental leave policies, subsidised childcare options and flexible work arrangements.

Participating in mentoring programs and financial literacy initiatives can empower women to make informed financial decisions and build stronger financial futures. It's also essential for women to be knowledgeable about their superannuation (pension) contributions, including understanding how and where their superannuation is being deposited and tracking it as they change jobs. There are insane statistics about unclaimed superannuation of people who have no idea they are owed it.

This can help ensure they are receiving the full benefits they are entitled to and can make informed decisions about their retirement savings. These efforts not only benefit individual women but contribute to a broader push for gender equality in the workplace and society at large. Advocating for equal pay and pension rights is also essential. While progress has been made in many countries, across the globe, women are underpaid in all these areas.

Financial literacy programmes are also essential to equip women with the knowledge and skills to navigate their financial futures effectively. By addressing these issues comprehensively, women can work towards more equitable opportunities throughout their work lives and retirement.

Beware of the Pink Tax: Gender and Financial Equity
The 'pink tax' refers to the extra costs often associated with products and services explicitly marketed to women. Awareness of these gender-based price disparities and conscious purchasing decisions can help you save money and promote financial equity. Literature exploring gender disparities in wealth, such as *Why Women Are Poorer Than Men* by Annabelle Williams, can offer valuable insights into building financial literacy and making excellent financial decisions.

Psychological Aspects of Money
We are often influenced by how our families view money and wealth. Understanding this can help you create a harmonious relationship with money. By educating yourself about financial principles, you can overcome inherited biases, beliefs or blocks and make more rational and productive decisions.

Being Financially Savvy: Making Informed Decisions
Financial savviness involves making informed investment decisions, managing debt and planning. By staying informed about financial markets and seeking professional advice when needed, you can make wise choices that help your long-term economic health. Many school leavers receive a credit card in the mail with a usable advance. If they are not careful, they can owe fortunes quickly, falling victim to the tyranny of debt.

Financial Wisdom from Experts

Achieving and keeping youthful vigour and financial security go hand in hand. By becoming financially literate and making excellent financial decisions, you can reduce stress, gain greater control over your life and secure a brighter future for yourself and your family. Financial health is not only about wealth; it's about empowerment and peace of mind. Teaching financial literacy to your family can help maintain and grow family wealth. If you are in a position where it's important to consider transferring assets to the next generation, ensure you have a will and consider establishing trusts. Regularly update your estate plan to reflect changes in your financial and family circumstances. Discuss financial goals, share budgeting and saving knowledge, and encourage good financial habits in younger generations.

The less stress you have about providing for yourself and your loved ones, the longer you will enjoy youthful fortitude, health and vitality.

Financial Literature for All

I am not a financial guru, but there are books to educate everyone about financial practices that will improve lives and lifestyles. Scott Pape's *The Barefoot Investor*, Robert Kiyosaki's *Rich Dad Poor Dad* and Tony Robbins' financial trilogy, *Money Master the Game: Seven Simple Steps to Financial Freedom* (2014); *Unshakeable: Your Financial Freedom Playbook* (2017); and *The Holy Grail of Investing* (2024) are essential reading for those interested in securing their financial future. Robert Kiyosaki even has a book for teens: *Rich Dad, Poor Dad for Teens*. Drawing wisdom from the writings of financial experts can start in adolescence. It makes sense to start your children early.

Final Words

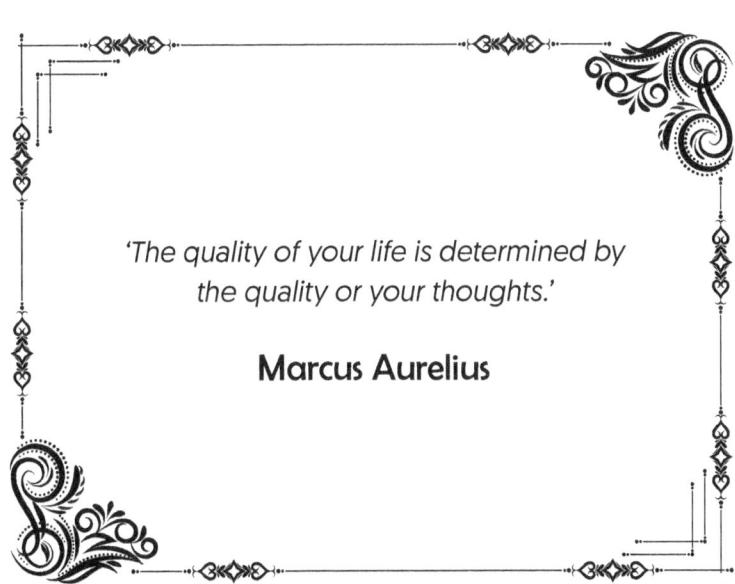

'The quality of your life is determined by the quality or your thoughts.'

Marcus Aurelius

Austin Tang has an analogy which resonates with me:

You are holding a cup of coffee when someone bumps into you, spilling your coffee everywhere. Why did you spill the coffee? Your answer: 'Because someone bumped into me!'

Wrong answer. You spilt the coffee because there was coffee in your cup. Had there been tea in the cup, you would have spilt tea. Whatever is inside the cup is what will spill out.

Therefore, whatever is inside you will come out when life shakes you (which it does).

Ask yourself, 'What's in my cup?' When life gets tough, what spills over? Joy, gratitude, peace and humility? Or anger, bitterness, a victim mentality and quitting tendencies?

Life provides the cup, and you choose how to fill it.

Apply a positive mindset to ageing, appreciate your achievements, and recognise the impact of your actions. Though seemingly unnoticed by many, your life holds immense value in bringing happiness and positively impacting lives within and beyond your family.

As I said at the start of this book, no-one can hurry up and get young. You can embrace the multifaceted journey to youthful ageing at any stage. This book will help you enhance your sense of vitality no matter what age you are. I also hope you will help young children and teenagers embrace these pathways, ideas and strategies to improve their lives and livelihoods.

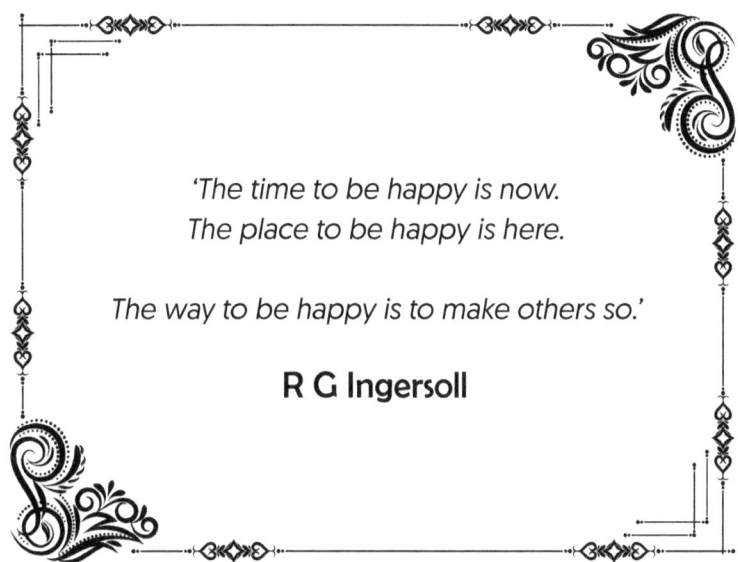

'The time to be happy is now.
The place to be happy is here.

The way to be happy is to make others so.'

R G Ingersoll

Although our lives are transient, we all leave spiritual footprints. No life is insignificant. You live for yourself and those around you; no-one else can do it like you do. Your impact and your legacy are invaluable, enduring and unique.

I will leave you with this poem:

You Start Dying Slowly

You start dying slowly
If you do not travel,
If you do not read,
If you do not listen to the sounds of life,
If you do not appreciate yourself.

You start dying slowly
When you kill your self-esteem,
When you do not let others help you.

You start dying slowly
If you become a slave of your habits,
Walking every day on the same paths …
If you do not change your routine,
If you do not wear different colours
Or you do not speak to those you don't know.

You start dying slowly
If you avoid feeling passion
And their turbulent emotions;
Those which make your eyes glisten
And your heart beat fast.

You start dying slowly
If you do not change your life when you are not satisfied with your job, or with your love,
If you do not risk what is safe for the uncertain,
If you do not go after a dream,
If you do not allow yourself, at least once in your lifetime, to run away from sensible advice …

Martha Medeiros
(Brazilian Poet)

References

Belsky, J., Caspi, A., Moffitt, T. E., & Poulton, R. (2020). *The Origins of You - How Childhood Shapes Later Life.* Massachusetts: Harvard University Press.

Clear, J. (2018). *Atomic Habits: An Easy & Proven Way to Build Good Habits & Break Bad Ones.* Century Trade.

Diamandis, P., Robbins, T., & Hariri, R. (2022). *Life Force: How New Breakthroughs in Precision Medicine Can Transform the Quality of Your Life & Those You Love.* Simon and Schuster.

Dweck, C. (2017). *Mindset - Updated Edition: Changing The Way You Think To Fulfil Your Potential.* Robinson.

Foster, V. (2024, April 24). *Artificial Sweeteners Could Seriously Damage Gut Health.* Retrieved from FORBES: https://www.forbes.com/sites/victoriaforster/2024/04/25/artificial-sweetener-can-seriously-damage-gut-according-to-new-study/#:~:text=The%20new%20study%20published%20in,according%20to%20the%20research%20team.

Goleman, D. (1995). *Emotional Intelligence.* New York: Bantam.

Harvard Education. (2007, May 10). *The Impact of Early Adversity on Child Development (In Brief).* Retrieved from Center on the Developing Child: www.developingchild.harvard.edu.

Holden, R. (1998). *Laughter is the Best Medicine. The Healing Power of Happiness, Humour and Laughter.* HarperCollins.

Martino, J., Pegg, J., & Pegg Frates, E. (2015). The Connection Prescription: Using the Power of Social Interactions and Deep Desire for Connectedness to Empower Health and Wellness. *American Journal of Lifestyle Medicine*, 11(6) 466-475.

Parker, J. O. (2014). *Face - Exercises to Keep Your Face Youthful and Healthy.* Tidal.

Powell, P., & Munoz, M. (2016). Early Childhood Experiences and Their Link to the Life Trajectories of Children. In *Social Justice Instruction* (pp. 117 - 128). 10.1007/978-3-319-12349-3_11.

Robbins, M. (2022). *The 5 Second Rule: Transform your Life, Work, and Confidence with Everyday Courage.* Savio Republic.

Shaver, P. R., & Mikulincer, M. (2012). Beyond illusions and defence: Exploring the possibilities and limits of human autonomy and responsibility through self-determination theory. In R. M. Ryan, N. Legate, C. P. Niemiec, & E. L. Deci, *Meaning, Mortality and Choice - The Social Psychology of Existential Concerns* (pp. 215-233). American Psychological Association.

Short Stories. (2024, May 1). *The Ant and the Grasshopper.* Retrieved from Short Stories: https://www.eastoftheweb.com/short-stories/UBooks/AntGra.shtml

Stiles, K. (2021, May 10). *The Importance of Connection.* Retrieved from PsychCentral: https://psychcentral.com/lib/the-importance-of-connection

Swan, N. (2022). *So You Want to Live Younger Longer?* Hachette.

Tracy, B. (2013). *Eat That Frog!: Get More of the Important Things Done - Today!* Hodder Press.

World Bank. (2024, March 25). *Education Overview.* Retrieved from World Bank: https://www.worldbank.org/en/topic/education/overview

About the Author

Lili-Ann's journey began in the vibrant city of Johannesburg, South Africa, where she lived with her parents, Bob and Bee, and her siblings, Helene and Martin. With her father's work in the gold mines, the family frequently relocated, turning each new place into an adventure. From a young age, Lili-Ann cherished moments with her grandparents and discovered a love for ballet and piano lessons. Inspired by her favourite author, Enid Blyton, she entertained her siblings with imaginative, made-up stories.

While she was at university, Lili-Ann met Pierre, the love of her life. Together, they built a joyful and fulfilling life in South Africa with their two children, Sean and Candice. Lili-Ann's career took off as she specialised in early childhood education, finding immense satisfaction in shaping young minds. As a late-blooming athlete, she earned Springbok national colours for racewalking in South Africa, reflecting her passion for an active lifestyle.

In 1998, a significant chapter began when Lili-Ann and her family moved to Australia. Embracing their new home, they forged strong friendships and immersed themselves in various activities, all while keeping cherished ties with lifelong friends from their youth. Their adventures took them across Europe and America, with skiing emerging as a beloved family holiday tradition.

More recently, Lili-Ann has added 'author' to her list of accomplishments. She has published *'The Power of Play – Master Seven Learning Zones'* for educators, and *Roots and Wings*, a guide for parents. And you're holding her third book, *Lifelong Vitality – Twelve Pathways to Ageing Youthfully*. Her early life experiences, vivid imagination and deep-seated passion for education continue to inspire her creative and professional endeavours.

Notes

www.ingramcontent.com/pod-product-compliance
Lightning Source LLC
Chambersburg PA
CBHW040108100526
44584CB00029BA/3935